NWO3001244   SAAP/04   £24.95

D1610472

WITHDRAWN

N 0115427 3

Behavioural Approaches in
Neuropsychological Rehabilitation

Behavioural Approaches in Neuropsychological Rehabilitation

Optimising Rehabilitation Procedures

Barbara A. Wilson

Medical Research Council Cognition and Brain Sciences Unit, Cambridge and The Oliver Zangwill Centre Ely, UK

Camilla M. Herbert

The Brain Injury Rehabilitation Trust, Burgess Hill, West Sussex, UK

Agnes Shiel

Faculty of Medicine and Health, NUI Galway, Ireland

NEWMAN COLLEGE
BARTLEY GREEN
BIRMINGHAM B32 3NT
CLASS   617·481
BARCODE 01154213
AUTHOR NIL

Ψ Psychology Press
Taylor & Francis Group

HOVE AND NEW YORK

First published 2003
by Psychology Press
27 Church Road, Hove, East Sussex BN3 2FA

Simultaneously published in the USA and Canada
by Psychology Press
29 West 35th Street, New York NY 10001

Psychology Press is a part of the Taylor & Francis Group

Copyright © 2003 Psychology Press

Typeset in Times by Graphicraft Limited, Hong Kong
Printed and bound in Great Britain by Biddles Ltd, Guildford and King's Lynn
Cover design by Hybert Design

All rights reserved. No part of this book may be reprinted or reproduced or
utilised in any form or by any electronic, mechanical, or other means, now
known or hereafter invented, including photocopying and recording, or in
any information storage or retrieval system, without permission in writing
from the publishers.

Every effort has been made to ensure that the advice and information in this
book is true and accurate at the time of going to press. However, neither the
publisher nor the authors can accept any legal responsibility or liability for
any errors or omissions that may be made. In the case of drug
administration, any medical procedure or the use of technical equipment
mentioned within this book, you are strongly advised to consult the
manufacturer's guidelines.

This publication has been produced with paper manufactured to strict
environmental standards and with pulp derived from sustainable forests.

British Library Cataloguing in Publication Data
A catalogue record for this book is available from the British Library

Library of Congress Cataloging-in-Publication Data
Wilson, Barbara A.
  Behavioural approaches in neuropsychological rehabilitation :
  optimising rehabilitation procedures / B.A. Wilson, C.M. Herbert,
  A. Shiel.— 1st ed.
      p.   cm.
  Includes bibliographical references and index.
    ISBN 1-84169-183-6 (hardcover)
    1. Brain damage—Patients—Rehabilitation. 2. Clinical
neuropsychology. I. Herbert, C. M. (Camilla M.), 1962– II. Shiel, A.
(Agnes), 1959– III. Title.
RC387.5.W5448 2003
617.4'810443—dc21   2003005281

ISBN 1-84169-183-6

Contents

Series preface

Rehabilitation is a process whereby people, who have been impaired by injury or illness, work together with health service staff and others to achieve their optimum level of physical, psychological, social, and vocational well-being (McLellan, 1991). It includes all measures aimed at reducing the impact of handicapping and disabling conditions and at enabling disabled people to return to their most appropriate environment (WHO, 1986; Wilson, 1997). It also includes attempts to alter impairment in underlying cognitive and brain systems by the provision of systematic, planned experience to the damaged brain (Robertson & Murre, 1999). The above views apply also to neuropsychological rehabilitation, which is concerned with the assessment, treatment, and natural recovery of people who have sustained an insult to the brain.

Neuropsychological rehabilitation is influenced by a number of fields both from within and without psychology. Neuropsychology, behavioural psychology, and cognitive psychology have each played important roles in the development of current rehabilitation practice. So too have findings from studies of neuroplasticity, linguistics, geriatric medicine, neurology, and other fields. Our discipline, therefore, is not confined to one conceptual framework; rather, it has a broad theoretical base.

We hope that this broad base is reflected in the modular handbook series. The first book was by Roger Barker and Stephen Dunnett which set the scene by talking about "Neural repair, transplantation and rehabilitation". The second title, by Josef Zihl, addressed visual disorders after brain injury. Forthcoming titles include volumes on specific cognitive functions such as language, memory, and motor skills, together with social and personality aspects of neuropsychological rehabilitation and behavioural approaches to rehabilitation. Other titles will follow as this is the kind of handbook that can be added to over the years.

Although each volume will be based on a strong theoretical foundation relevant to the topic in question, the main thrust of a majority of the books will be the development of practical, clinical methods of rehabilitation arising out of this research enterprise.

The series is aimed at neuropsychologists, clinical psychologists, and other rehabilitation specialists such as occupational therapists, speech and language pathologists, rehabilitation physicians, and other disciplines involved in the rehabilitation of people with brain injury.

Neuropsychological rehabilitation is at an exciting stage in its development. On the one hand, we have a huge growth of interest in functional imaging techniques to tell us about the basic processes going on in the brain. On the other hand, the past few years have seen the introduction of a number of theoretically driven approaches to cognitive rehabilitation from the fields of language, memory, attention, and perception. In addition to both the above, there is a growing recognition from health services that rehabilitation is an integral part of a health care system. Of course, alongside the recognition of the need for rehabilitation is the view that any system has to be evaluated. To those of us working with brain-injured people including those with dementia, there is a feeling that things are moving forward. This series, we hope, is one reflection of this move and the integration of theory and practice.

REFERENCES

McLellan, D. L. (1991). Functional recovery and the principles of disability medicine. In M. Swash & J. Oxbury (Eds.), *Clinical neurology*. Edinburgh: Churchill Livingstone.

Robertson, I. H., & Murre, J. M. J. (1999). Rehabilitation of brain damage: Brain plasticity and principles of guided recovery. *Psychological Bulletin, 125*, 544–575.

Wilson, B. A. (1997). Cognitive rehabilitation: How it is and how it might be. *Journal of the International Neuropsychological Society, 3*, 487–496.

World Health Organisation (1986). Optimum care of disabled people. *Report of a WHO meeting*, Turku, Finland.

BARBARA A. WILSON
IAN H. ROBERTSON

Other titles available in this series:

Neural Repair, Transplantation and Rehabilitation
by Roger A. Barker & Stephen B. Dunnett

Rehabilitation of Visual Disorders After Brain Injury
by Joseph Zihl

Preface

This book describes approaches to rehabilitation for people with acquired brain injury. It is concerned with how methods from behavioural medicine can be adapted to alleviate cognitive, emotional, social, and personality problems. Although some of the people described in the book have mild behaviour problems, we do not focus on individuals with very severe disruptive behaviour disorders, such as those described by Wood and Eames (1981), as there is already a considerable literature concentrating on this group.

Like Levenkron (1987), we see behavioural approaches to rehabilitation as a "process of clinical reasoning" (p. 384) rather than a fixed set of techniques to be followed rigidly and adhered to, come what may. It is a process concerned with improving the everyday lives of people with acquired brain injury and their families, by enabling us to conceptualise, identify, and measure their problems, and to plan and implement programmes to reduce difficulties, increase strengths, and teach new skills. To a large extent, behavioural approaches involve the application of principles derived from learning theory, or from research in experimental or social psychology, to the remediation of human problems. Such approaches emphasise systematic evaluation of the applications (Franks & Wilson, 1975).

Kazdin and Hersen (1980, p. 287) suggested that followers of behaviour therapy have four main characteristics:

i) A strong commitment to the empirical evaluation of treatment and intervention techniques; ii) A general belief that therapeutic experiences must provide opportunities to learn adaptive or prosocial behaviour; iii) specification of treatment in operational and, hence, replicable terms; iv) Evaluation of treatment effects through multiple-response modalities with particular emphasis on overt behaviour.

It is our contention that these approaches are valuable in neuropsychological rehabilitation because they benefit assessment, treatment, and measurement of rehabilitation efficacy.

Despite the wide variety of strategies that have emerged from behavioural psychology and been applied to medical settings, they tend to share common themes. First, all are concerned with the development of reliable and valid assessment instruments. Pearce and Wardle (1989) believe these instruments are the hallmark of the behavioural scientist. Liaison with other disciplines is another characteristic of behavioural medicine. From the beginnings of behavioural psychology in learning disability to its wide application in many medical conditions such as diabetes, chronic pain, obesity, addiction, and brain injury, behavioural scientists frequently work in multidisciplinary and interdisciplinary teams, making such liaison crucially important to success. Second, all behavioural methods involve careful monitoring and evaluation of treatment efficacy. This is often done at the individual level and the widespread use of single-case experimental designs grew directly out of behavioural psychology (Wilson, 1987).

Although we concentrate on behavioural approaches in this book, we do not believe that the employment of behavioural methods in neuropsychological rehabilitation should be at the expense of other approaches. We need to incorporate models, knowledge, and assessment and treatment strategies from psychotherapy, cognitive neuropsychology, neuroplasticity, linguistics, and other fields. As Diller (1987) said, we need a broader theoretical base or several theoretical bases. It is vitally important that therapists do not become constrained by one theoretical framework, as this is unlikely to lead to the best rehabilitation practice for people who survive brain injury, whose needs are almost certainly going to warrant treatments informed by a whole range of varied approaches.

We would also like to say in this foreword that we regard behavioural approaches, applied properly, as benevolent and humane, and just as worthy of being so labelled as any other approach. For too long there has been a kind of intellectual cowardice that has found its expression in a denial of the use of behavioural methodologies, when in fact such approaches have been central to the work of the deniers themselves! We believe that such cowardice has its origins in an outdated Marxist critique that was fashionable in the 1960s and 1970s. Indeed, we would argue that behaviourism has been used by both Marxists and their opponents as a cudgel with which to beat each other, in what has always been an anti-intellectual battle that the authors of this book are happy to dismiss. In the end, any methodology can be used humanely, and this is dependent not on the approach but on the attitude of practitioners. Conversely, no approach, whatever its label, can claim to be more humane than any other. The important thing in neuropsychological rehabilitation is to have the well-being of the patient as the overarching goal, and we believe this is best achieved by working in cooperation with the patient (and relatives). Behavioural approaches seem to us to have a distinct advantage in providing programmes that can be easily understood and managed by therapists, patients, and relatives working closely together.

List of tables and figures

CHAPTER 1

A brief history of behavioural approaches in neuropsychological rehabilitation

In 1977, Lane published a detailed account of Itard's work with Victor, the Wild Boy of Aveyron, in the eighteenth century. Many of the methods adopted by Itard to teach Victor certain skills were later incorporated into behaviour modification techniques. Itard used approximations that today we would call shaping; he identified the component parts of complex activities and taught the individual parts that today we would call chaining; and he was concerned with limitation and generalisation, which are widely used today in the teaching of people with learning disability. Lane (1977) concludes that, "his [Itard's] armamentarium . . . anticipated that of modern behavioural modification by nearly two centuries" (p. 165).

Although they did not use the terms *behaviour therapy* or *behaviour modification*, Luria and colleagues employed behavioural techniques in their work with brain-injured people in the Soviet Union (Luria, 1963; Luria, Naydin, Tsvetkova, & Vinarskaya, 1969). They argued that following a brain lesion there is primary damage resulting in the death of neurons, and secondary damage due to the inhibition of intact neurons. They describe successful rehabilitation programmes based on the principles of de-inhibition. De-blocking or de-inhibiting secondary damage can be accomplished by combining pharmacological treatment with careful training procedures. Luria et al. believed that because the inhibition resulted from poor synaptic transmission, drugs modifying this transmission should be used. If, at the same time, patients were enabled to use residual powers and substitute these for the original, habitual way of carrying out an activity, then behavioural change could occur. The procedures described are similar to shaping procedures used today in behaviour therapy. In their 1969 paper, for example, Luria et al. describe Perelman's work with post-concussional deaf patients. These patients were asked to read sentences that were, at the same time, read aloud by a therapist. Of course the deafened patients could not hear the therapist but they could read with no trouble. Gradually, the written sentences were made less and less legible while the spoken sentences were always clearly pronounced. Those patients who possessed inhibited traces of hearing were gradually guided by the sound of the sentences and learned to "hear" the sounds even when the written word was illegible. As shaping can be defined as successive approximations to a final goal, these patients were being shaped to hear again.

One of the first people to describe explicitly and advocate the use of behavioural techniques with brain-injured adults was Goodkin (1966). He used operant conditioning to improve a number of skills including handwriting, machine operating, and wheelchair pushing with three stroke patients and one patient with Parkinson's disease. A further paper by Goodkin (1969) described how operant conditioning resulted in language improvement in a patient with dysphasia following a stroke.

The 1970s saw several reports of behavioural methods used with brain-injured adults. Taylor and Persons (1970) used social attention to (a) reinforce reading skills in a 22-year-old quadriplegic man, (b) reduce the number of complaints made by a 54-year-old woman with multiple sclerosis, and (c) extinguish psychotic speech in a 37-year-old quadriplegic man. All patients became easier for ward staff to manage. A similar approach with money as a reward was employed by Booraem and Seacat (1972) to reinforce exercising in brain-damaged adults in a general hospital. Zlutnick, Mayville, and Moffat (1975) were able to reduce the number of epileptic seizures sustained by a 17-year-old girl by interrupting the sequence of behaviours that led up to the seizure. Ince (1976), in his book on behaviour modification in rehabilitation, concentrated on the reduction of problem behaviours although he also included suggestions on how behaviour modification could be used in other areas of rehabilitation. Lincoln (1978) produced a short paper entitled "Behaviour modification in physiotherapy" describing three programmes designed to extend exercising in physiotherapy for one stroke and two head-injured patients. In the same year Series and Lincoln reported on the applications of behaviour therapy to people with brain injury (Series & Lincoln, 1978). Lincoln and colleagues later published work on behaviour therapy as an aid to treating language disorders (Lincoln & Pickersgill, 1984; Lincoln, Pickersgill, Hankey, & Hilton, 1982).

Others who touched on aspects of cognitive remediation were Goodkin (1969), and Diller and his colleagues working with right hemisphere stroke patients exhibiting visuoperceptual and visuospatial problems (Diller & Weinberg, 1977; Weinberg et al., 1979). Although Diller and his colleagues did not describe their methods as behavioural, in many ways they incorporated behavioural principles in that they thought it important to establish the nature of the problem, obtain a baseline, and start training with easy tasks before progressing to more complex ones. They also point out the importance of providing cues and environmental supports in the early stages before progressing to the more complex ones. Feedback and evaluation are also considered to be crucial aspects of training. Thus they were following the behavioural principles of task analysis, observation and recording of the problem behaviours, shaping, reinforcement, and monitoring or evaluation of treatment effectiveness, all of which are components of behavioural assessment and treatment programmes (Yule & Carr, 1987).

It was in the 1980s that behavioural techniques began to be applied to cognitive problems in earnest. In a later book by Ince (1980), Diller wrote a chapter on cognitive rehabilitation describing the techniques established during the 1970s (Diller, 1980). Wilson (1981) published a survey of behavioural treatments carried out at a brain injury rehabilitation centre. These included programmes for people with memory, perceptual, and language disorders. Around the same time, Miller (1980) discussed the application of psychological (including behavioural) techniques to the treatment of people with central nervous system damage. Miller emphasised that treatment should be concerned with the amelioration of deficits rather than attempting to restore lost functioning. He expanded these ideas in a later book (Miller, 1984) in which he stated that amelioration helps an individual to function as well as possible despite handicaps, whereas restitution implies the recovery or regaining of lost abilities which, in his view, is not possible. This debate continues today and, while it is likely that Miller's views are correct for the majority of patients, there are documented cases where some restoration or restitution of functioning does appear to have taken place despite permanent organic damage (Wilson, 1998).

In the last 20 years or so more papers have appeared reporting the use of behavioural approaches in neuropsychology (see, for example, Alderman, 1996; Bellus, Kost, Vergo, & Dinezza, 1998; Wilson, 1988, 1999; Wilson & Robertson, 1992, and others). These publications discuss several reasons why behavioural methods are suitable and effective for people with brain injury, and many of these we list below.

(1) There are many treatment techniques to either decrease problem behaviours or increase desirable behaviours that can be adapted or modified for use with our patient population.
(2) The underlying theoretical frameworks of behavioural approaches come from a number of fields including learning theory, neuroplasticity, information processing, linguistics, psychiatry, and so forth. This richness and complexity of theoretical support and clinical treatment means that behavioural medicine can be applied to a wide range of patients, problems, and situations.
(3) The targets, aims, and goals of therapy are made clear from the beginning of each programme. Unlike, say, interpretative psychotherapy, which arrives at its specification at the *end* of therapy, behavioural approaches specify the goals at the beginning of the process. Furthermore, the goals are explicit, small, and usually easy to achieve.

(4) Fourth, assessment and treatment are frequently inseparable in behavioural treatment programmes, unlike other treatments. Neuropsychological or cognitive assessments, for example, are typically unrelated or indirectly related to the treatment. Poor scores on intelligence tests or memory tests are not targeted for treatment; we do not teach people to pass these tests. The scores are important in helping us to understand a person's cognitive strengths and weaknesses, and to plan our intervention appropriately, but they do not inform us in any detail about everyday problems, how families cope, what brain-injured people want to achieve, or how environments may affect behaviour. For such information we must employ behavioural assessments that are often part of the treatment strategy itself.

(5) Behavioural interventions are continuously monitored. Without measurement we are in danger of giving subjective or intuitive opinions about behavioural change or treatment effectiveness. Some of the most valuable evaluation techniques in neuropsychological rehabilitation are the single-case experimental designs developed in the field of behavioural medicine. These designs help us tease out whether change is due to natural recovery (or some other non-specific factor) or to our intervention.

(6) Within a behavioural approach it is possible to individualise treatment, and this is particularly helpful for some brain-injured patients who will probably not respond to "packaged treatment" such as computerised cognitive retraining or memory exercises. These "packaged" programmes have not been designed to take into account the complex mixture of cognitive, social, emotional, and behavioural problems of brain-injured people and may have not been properly evaluated. In contrast, behavioural programmes typically take into account the biological condition of the individual, precipitating events, consequences of events, social factors, and the environment in which the individual is functioning. "Lesions in the same general areas do not always show the same symptoms and potential for restitution" (Finger & Stein, 1982, p. 336), thus a more individually oriented approach to therapy is called for, "one that would take into account not only features of the lesion, but factors such as motivation, age, experiential history, and the status of the rest of the brain."

(7) Behavioural approaches provide a set of principles and a structure to follow when designing treatment programmes. Task analysis, goal setting, appropriate and detailed assessments, recording, monitoring, and evaluating the programme provide sound guidelines for psychologists, therapists, or teachers to follow.

(8) Behavioural approaches have been successful, as we demonstrate in later chapters of this book.

To expand on the view expressed in the foreword, we believe that the employment of behavioural methods in rehabilitation should not be at the expense of other approaches. Most British neuropsychologists or clinical psychologists working in the field of brain injury rehabilitation will draw on several fields, methodologies, and theoretical models from their training. Cognitive psychology provides models of memory, language, perception, attention, and so forth to help us understand and explain related phenomena; neuropsychology provides us with an understanding of the organisation of the brain; and behavioural psychology provides us with assessment and treatment methods to try to change behaviour. In addition, we are likely to be influenced by cognitive-behaviour therapy and psychotherapy to change attitudes and reduce emotional distress; findings from neuroplasticity to help understand and predict recovery; linguistics to help remediate language disorders; phenomenology for the understanding of individual differences—and influences abound from other related fields. The strength of neuropsychological rehabilitation is that it is *not* confined to or constrained by one theoretical framework. We would argue that such constraint is dangerous, in rehabilitation. No single approach can help us understand in totality the nature of our client's deficits, or inform us as to how best to select or apply appropriate treatment and management strategies; no approach on its own can succeed in reducing all the consequences of brain injury, or enable patients and their families to achieve all their everyday goals. Instead we need to combine theories, methodologies, and approaches from a number of fields in order to encourage optimum levels of cognitive, emotional, and physical rehabilitation.

Similarly, no single approach can claim to be more benevolent than any other, although it would be true to say that there have been occasions when opponents of behavioural approaches have defended themselves as being more caring of the patient, as though this was inherently part of their philosophy or methodology. In fact a caring attitude can and indeed must be shown towards the patient at all times by each therapist, irrespective of treatment strategies. Caring for the patient is as much part of behaviourism as it is part of any approach, and no one has the right to claim a greater share of benevolence as though it were intrinsic to their philosophy, or a natural part of their theory or practice.

CHAPTER 2

Assessment for rehabilitation: Integrating information from neuropsychological and behavioural assessment

BACKGROUND

An acceptable definition of assessment, for the purpose of this chapter, is that offered by Sundberg and Tyler (1962) when they describe it as ". . . the systematic collection, organisation and interpretation of information about a person and his (or her) situation" (p. 8). Of the several ways of obtaining this information, the two most relevant for rehabilitation of people with brain injury are assessment procedures from neuropsychological and behavioural disciplines. Both approaches have important and complementary roles to play in assessing the nature of cognitive impairments, remaining capabilities, and the problems likely to be confronted in daily life by the person with brain injury.

Neuropsychology is the study of the relationship between brain and behaviour, and neuropsychological testing is mostly (although not solely) concerned with assessing *cognitive* functions. Other areas of human functioning, involving motor skills, and physical, emotional, and social behaviour are also frequently adversely affected as a result of injury to the brain. In order to assess damage in these areas we can employ investigative techniques based on behavioural theory, although, again, we need to add the proviso that in some cases neuropsychological testing may also be appropriate.

Behaviour can be defined as any observable or measurable response made by an organism. Behavioural assessments are typically concerned with identifying and measuring problem behaviours encountered in the everyday lives of those who have suffered injury to the brain. Because assessments are conducted in order to answer particular questions, the nature of the questions posed in

7

any particular case will determine the assessment tool or procedure adopted. Neuropsychological and behavioural assessments answer different questions, both sets of which are required in rehabilitation.

NEUROPSYCHOLOGICAL ASSESSMENT

Examples of questions that can often be answered with a reasonable degree of accuracy by neuropsychological tests or assessment procedures are as follows:

- Is this person intellectually impaired?
- What is the predicted level of premorbid functioning for this person?
- What kind of language/reading/perceptual/memory disorder does this person have?
- Which cognitive skills remain intact or appear less damaged?
- How does this person compare with others of the same age or others with the same diagnosis?
- Is the score on a particular test in the abnormal range?
- Is failure on a particular test due to a disorder of comprehension, recognition, planning, or memory?
- Is the person faking or exaggerating problems?

Numerous theoretical influences might come into play when answering these questions. For example, psychometric assessments are based on statistical analysis and include measures of reliability, validity, and performance of a selected sample of a given population. Anastasi (1988) provides a succinct account of the characteristics of psychological tests. The Revised Wechsler Scales (Wechsler, 1981, 1987) are examples of tests influenced by psychometry.

Theoretical models from cognitive neuropsychology have led to the development of specialised and sophisticated assessment tools. For example, models of reading (Coltheart, 1985; Patterson, 1994) have led to systematic and careful assessment of the ability to read parts of speech, words of different length, nonsense words, irregular versus regular words, words acquired at different ages, and highly imageable versus abstract words. These models enable us to understand and explain such phenomena as the ability of some subjects to read nouns but not verbs, or words that are spelled regularly but not irregularly, or concrete but not abstract words.

The working memory model (Baddeley & Hitch, 1974) is another example of a theoretical cognitive model that has influenced neuropsychological assessment procedures. As a result of this model, clinicians are now more likely to assess separately those individual components specified in the model known as the central executive, the visuospatial sketchpad, and the phonological loop. Furthermore, the model helps to predict or explain the differences between people with short-term and long-term memory deficits.

Localisation studies have encouraged other approaches to assessment whereby, for example, the examiner attempts to assess deficits in the right and left hemispheres, and the frontal, temporal, parietal, and occipital lobes. The Halstead–Reitan Battery (Halstead, 1947; Reitan & Davison, 1974) is such an approach, and was originally used to discriminate between patients with frontal lobe lesions and normal control subjects.

The identification of neuropsychological syndromes such as agnosia and apraxia require a different set of guidelines that encourage the examiner to eliminate or exclude other explanations for the disorder. Although apraxia, for example, is a disorder of movement, it is not due to paralysis, weakness, or failure to understand the task, and the examiner must therefore exclude motor and comprehension deficits in order to diagnose the deficit.

Lezak (1995) discusses both theoretical and practical considerations in her comprehensive account of the characteristics of neuropsychological assessment.

BEHAVIOURAL ASSESSMENT

While it is true that the discipline of neuropsychology has provided important and sophisticated understanding of cognitive problems such as those described above, it is also true that the discipline cannot, at least as yet, directly help us find answers to other important questions in the field of rehabilitation. Standardised or traditional neuropsychological tests cannot readily answer questions such as the following:

- How is the person with brain injury and the family affected by the cognitive or neuropsychological problems identified?
- Can the client return home or continue with schooling?
- What coping strategies could be employed by the person with neuropsychological deficits?
- Which problems should be targeted in rehabilitation?
- What treatment methods should be employed?
- How should efficacy of treatment be measured?

In order to plan effective rehabilitation we need answers to such questions. People with brain injury and their carers are more concerned with problems that prevent them from coping in everyday situations than with whether or not they can score well on neuropsychological tests. Clients may be worried about getting lost when driving, losing belongings, or forgetting to take essential medicines. We do not *treat* an inability to perform a particular neuropsychological test, and improvement on such a test is not, as a rule, a good way of measuring real-life outcomes. People can and do improve on standardised tests yet remain unable to function in their own homes. Conversely, they can improve functionally without getting better on standardised tests. The main characteristics of

TABLE 2.1
Main characteristics of neuropsychological and behavioural assessments

Standardised (neuropsychological)	Functional (behavioural)
Tells us what a person *has* (e.g., amnesia)	Tells us what a person *does* (e.g., forgets people's names)
Behaviour is seen as a *sign* of the disorder (e.g., cannot do paired-associate learning—a sign of amnesia)	Behaviour is seen as a *sample* (e.g., tester samples the patient's remembering or forgetting performance)
Samples *one* situation (e.g., how a patient performs in the psychologist's office)	Samples *many* situations (e.g., observes patient in OT, PT)
Diagnostic	Helps select treatment
Indirect relationship to treatment	Direct relationship to treatment
Prior to (and sometimes post) treatment	Assessment and treatment continuous

Both types of assessment are useful as they provide complementary information

standardised (neuropsychological) and functional (behavioural) assessments are summarised in Table 2.1.

One way to address the more practical problems encountered in daily living, and to measure treatment effectiveness, is to employ behavioural assessment techniques that have developed from learning theory and behaviour modification. An essential prerequisite of this approach is to define precisely what is to be measured. Take the example of an occupational therapist who has asked the neuropsychologist for help in improving the poor concentration of a young man who has sustained a head injury. Before a start can be made, one has to ask how "poor concentration" is to be defined. It might be that the man is easily distractible, or finds difficulty in attending to what the therapist is saying, or has an immediate memory deficit that is manifested in repeated requests for repetition of instructions. It is possible that anxiety is an underlying condition leading to poor concentration.

The first step in attempting to understand the concerns of the therapist is to discuss the original observations leading to the request for help. Such discussion might lead to the development of one or more hypotheses that can be tested and either confirmed or rejected. Let us suppose the man is unable to work for more than 2 or 3 minutes before vacating a seat or talking to fellow patients. This behaviour might be measured by recording the number of times he leaves his seat during a therapy session, the number of times he talks to someone, and/or the number of minutes spent on a task before becoming distracted. Whatever the decision, it is essential that the behaviour is observable or rateable, and is clearly and unambiguously defined. This approach requires direct observation either in the natural setting of the occupational therapist's office or in a simulation of that setting.

Another choice for the psychologist is to decide whether to use dependent or independent observers. The former are those who are naturally in the situation (in this case the occupational therapist), the latter are specially recruited for the observation. The main advantage of dependent observers is that they are more likely to be accepted by the person being observed. However, dependent observers may be too busy being part of the usual situation to be able to observe effectively. While the main advantage of using independent observers is that they have time to monitor closely the person and the behaviour in question, the disadvantage of their presence is that they are not a natural part of the usual setting and may therefore cause changes in the behaviour being observed. A decision on these matters can be arrived at only after weighing the pros and cons in the light of such issues as the practicalities of the working environment, time restrictions, and the nature of the behaviour being observed.

Further choices have to be made before recording methods are selected. A frequency recording counts the number of times a behaviour occurs during a given period. Indirect measures might involve counting the products of behaviour, such as the number of lines typed in an occupational therapy session. Interval recording (i.e., observing whether or not the behaviour occurs during predetermined intervals) is useful when the behaviour in question is of such a high frequency that it is not practical to count every instance. Instead, one may observe for short bursts of a similar length during a longer period of, say, half an hour. Time sampling is similar, but here recordings are made at a particular point in time, say every half hour on the half hour, to see whether the behaviour is occurring at that moment. Duration recording is employed when measuring the length of time a patient engages in a particular behaviour.

In addition to paper-and-pencil recording sheets there are a number of useful instruments for temporal recording, including hand or wrist counters, stop watches, or devices that are operated directly by the subject's own movements. Some subtle behaviour changes can be detected only by special instruments that can record the voice or changes in muscle tension, posture, position of the head, and so forth. Also of course audio and video recordings have enabled the recording of behaviour that can be scored at a later date, and these can also be combined with electrical counters that enable frequency counts. Such instruments can save time and effort, yield data on subtle events, and lead to greater inter-rater reliability.

Despite these developments in recording, there is little doubt that direct observation is time consuming and not always feasible. An alternative way of obtaining behavioural information is to rely on self-report procedures such as questionnaires, checklists, or rating scales. Although these have the advantages of being quick and capable of focusing narrowly on specific behaviours, they rely on opinions rather than actualities. In other words, what people *think* they do may be quite different from what they actually do! Staff and family members can be useful information providers and sometimes important insights are discovered by reviewing discrepancies between a patient's self-report and that of a relative or staff member. It should be remembered, however that carers' views may also be subject to bias so a discrepancy does not necessarily mean lack of insight from the patient. Once again the pros and cons of direct observation of behaviour versus self-report measures have to be weighed before reaching a decision. Often one can use a combination of the two.

INTEGRATING INFORMATION FROM BOTH DISCIPLINES

Combining the knowledge gained from neuropsychological assessment and behavioural observation and measurement makes sense. The disciplines should be regarded as complementary and not mutually exclusive. Given the acknowledged gaps in our understanding of the effects of brain injury, the clearest attainable picture of a patient's abilities, impairments, behaviour, and social interaction will be drawn from a combination of knowledge gained from both disciplines. In the example above, the head-injured man suffering from poor concentration was assessed on measures of attention, immediate and delayed memory, perception, language, reading, executive functions, and reasoning. Knowledge thereby gained was combined with that obtained from behavioural measures of his problems as observed in real-life situations, and a more informed rehabilitation programme was thus inaugurated. A description of this patient, his results from both kinds of assessment, and his subsequent rehabilitation programme can be found in Wilson (1991a).

ECOLOGICALLY VALID TESTS

A recent development in the design of assessment tools has been the introduction of what have become known as ecologically valid tests. These represent an attempt to bridge neuropsychological and behavioural approaches. Basically, these tests aim to mimic real-life behaviours in test situations. One reason for assessing people with brain injury is to predict future behaviour in new situations. Neuropsychological tests may do this indirectly even though they are not designed primarily for this purpose. For example, stroke patients who make a large number of omission errors on cancellation tests are likely to have more accidents than patients who make few omissions. The reason for this is that cancellation tests are sensitive to unilateral neglect, a disorder in which patients fail to respond, orient, or attend to one part of space. Similarly, poor performance on a block design task may be associated with poor dressing skills as both involve visuospatial functioning. Nevertheless, there is not a direct or obvious relationship between test performance and real-life functioning. While behavioural assessments, on the other hand, do reflect, and are therefore more likely to predict, real-life performance, they are not always easy to set up and can be very time consuming.

Because the relatively new tests described in this section are standardised in the traditional manner and also map directly on to real-life tasks, their ecological validity can be demonstrated: that is to say, they can predict real-life behaviour. One of the first of these instruments to be developed was the *Test of Functional Communication for Aphasic Adults* (Holland, 1980). *The Rivermead Behavioural Memory Test* appeared in 1985 (Wilson, Cockburn, & Baddeley, 1985), followed in recent years by the *Cognitive Competency Test* (Wang & Ennis, 1986), the *Behavioural Inattention Test* (Wilson, Cockburn, & Halligan, 1987), *The Autobiographical Memory Interview* (Kopelman, Wilson, & Baddeley, 1990), and *The Test of Everyday Attention* (Robertson, Ward, Ridgeway, & Nimmo-Smith, 1994). A recent test in a rapidly growing tradition is the *Behavioural Assessment of the Dysexecutive Syndrome* (Wilson, Alderman, Burgess, Emslie, & Evans, 1996). This is a test designed to predict everyday problems arising from deficits in executive functioning or frontal lobe damage.

Such tests are useful adjuncts to full assessment when planning rehabilitation for people with brain injury. They combine the scientific rigour of standardised tests, aimed at identifying cognitive strengths and weaknesses, with observational or self-report measures that aim to assess more qualitative abilities involving insight, motivation, coping styles, and so forth. Other important points to note about these tests are that they are usually quickly administered, thus saving precious time for therapists and avoiding frustration among clients, and they address issues that are recognised as important by patients, relatives, and professional staff. One of the disadvantages is that they do not specify in sufficient detail the nature of the everyday problems to be targeted for intervention. So some direct observational or self-report measures will, as a rule, need to be incorporated into the assessments. In the Rivermead Behavioural Memory Test, for example, the test will give us a fairly good idea as to whether or not the person is likely to experience memory problems, but we will need to specify in greater detail just which problems the family and client needs help with.

USING INFORMATION FROM ASSESSMENTS TO PLAN REHABILITATION PROGRAMMES

In the United Kingdom and many other countries assessment takes place following a referral. This referral is often made by a consultant or other medical person, less frequently by a therapist or an organisation such as Headway, or the Brain Injury Association. Whoever is responsible for the referral should ensure that the assessor is fully informed of the referral requirements, and should avoid general and unhelpful requests such as, "Psychometry please" or "Please advise on management". Precise questions are favoured by the assessor, such as, "Is this woman's failure to learn how to transfer due to comprehension, perceptual, or memory deficits?". More typically, a referral might ask, "Is this woman in the early stages of Alzheimer's disease?" or "Please suggest how best to manage this man's memory problems".

In some cases the referral question might be answered with standardised tests alone. For example, the woman who could not learn to transfer was very aphasic following a left hemisphere stroke. Her physiotherapist asked the assessor the above question concerning comprehension, perceptual, and memory deficits, and the assessment found that she was very severely impaired on all tests of language and reading. She also performed badly on the Rivermead Behavioural Memory Test, even when compared with other dysphasic patients. However, her basic perceptual functioning on parts of the *Visual Object and Space Perception Battery* (Warrington & James, 1991) was normal. The assessors' conclusions were that failure to learn how to transfer was probably due to both comprehension and memory deficits. An *aide memoire* was provided in the form of a small card on which was drawn, as a series of cartoons, the steps required to transfer. The woman was taken through the steps as presented on the card. Each time, this procedure was accompanied by a demonstration of the correct movement and after several demonstrations the woman learned to refer to the card herself when transferring.

When treatment is to follow assessment, however, it is more usual for a combination of standardised and behavioural assessments to be administered. To illustrate the processes involved in such a combination of assessments, leading to the design of appropriate treatment programmes, their inauguration and subsequent effects, the following case study is offered.

Ted was referred by his speech therapist who reported that he was a "recovered Broca's aphasic" who was no longer able to read because he neglected the initial letters of words. Although neglect dyslexia is not uncommon after a *right* hemisphere stroke (Ellis, Flude, & Young, 1987; Riddoch, 1991), this man had an infarct in the territory of the *left* posterior cerebral artery with a right homonymous hemianopia.

In addition to a standardised speech and language assessment, which reported good verbal comprehension of even complex tasks and fluent, grammatical expressive language, Ted was given a basic neuropsychological assessment. His verbal IQ, as assessed by the WAIS, was 112 and his performance IQ was 90. He showed mild word-finding deficits in both object and picture naming. His everyday memory was in the average range when assessed on the Rivermead Behavioural Memory Test, and he was slow but showed no signs of neglect on the Behavioural Inattention Test. He was able to copy drawings accurately. Furthermore, his behaviour was not like that of a patient with neglect. He scanned appropriately and accurately, and he could "see" the initial letters of words as he pointed to them with his finger and said, "I can see them as well as you can, I just can't tell what it is." Perhaps an even more convincing argument against a neglect hypothesis was that Ted, with his left hemisphere damage, should have shown right-sided neglect if he was going to neglect at all.

Ted's inability to identify initial stimuli was restricted to letters and numbers. He could identify geometric shapes, so his problem was not due to a global deficit in the detection and identification of any element on the left of a horizontal display.

The next step was to analyse in more detail Ted's reading difficulties. Two unexpected findings showed that (a) he was more adept at reading long words as opposed to short, thus he could read words such as "astrocytoma" and "idiosyncrasy" but could not read words such as "sit" or "nose"; and (b) his performance was better when reading orthographically unusual words such as "yacht" than it was when reading words with a more common spelling such as "sight". The majority of his errors (67%) consisted of substitutions such as "fail" for "rail". Only 3% of his errors were deletions ("ear" for "pear"); 11% were substitutions and additions ("shall" for "fall"); 8% were additions before or after the initial letters ("spout" for "pout", "broom" for "boom"); and 11% were errors of other types ("purse" for "horse"). Ted also made errors on reading single letters: 23% of upper case and 42% of lower case were incorrect. He was better at reading text than letters or words, almost certainly because the context constrains possible options.

In this way we built up a fairly clear picture of Ted's cognitive functioning, through a combination of standardised tests and manipulations of stimuli. The behavioural assessment really came into play when we tried to find a treatment strategy. We systematically assessed Ted's response to different reading environments, thus illustrating the close relationship between behavioural assessment and behavioural treatment. Each treatment selection was based on a rationale. In most cases the treatment had been used successfully for people with neglect or with memory difficulties. Ted's virtually unique deficit meant we had no previous strategies to guide us.

We knew that Ted's reading problem was not due to poor eyesight or to unilateral visual neglect or word-finding difficulties. Several treatment approaches were tried. The first was to use an established neglect treatment of finding an anchor point (Diller & Weinberg, 1977; Riddoch & Humphries, 1994) whereby a thick red line is drawn to the left of the stimuli and neglect patients are taught to find this line first, before scanning the text. This failed to help Ted at all. Perhaps this was not surprising as he did not neglect the initial letter, he saw it but could not identify it.

The second treatment involved repetition of the initial letter in a word (e.g., "ssock") in the expectation that Ted could begin the word with the second letter and thus avoid or bypass his problem. This also failed, presumably because Ted was aware that English words rarely begin with two identical letters.

The third method involved placing an irrelevant stimulus in front of the word (e.g., "xmad") but once again we failed to help Ted because he realised the "x" was irrelevant, moved on to the true beginning of the word, the "m", and then typically read the word as "sad" or "bad".

At this point a colleague, Arnold Wilkins, saw Ted and persuaded him to read by looking through a narrow tube with a magnifying lens at one end. This had the effect of isolating letters or syllables from their surroundings. However, Ted disliked this method and we were unable to obtain sufficient data to evaluate its efficacy.

In the fifth method we attempted to teach letters to Ted by drawing in an identifying feature, so that "S" was drawn as an s-shaped snake. Ted showed poor learning at this, was very slow, and did not generalise from the drawn letter to letters in print.

Method number six involved expanding rehearsal (Landauer & Bjork, 1978). Ted was told the name of one letter (e.g., "b"), asked to repeat it immediately, then tested after 1 second, 2 seconds, 3 seconds, and so forth. Although he could retain one letter at a time if no other tasks were introduced, it proved impossible for him to retain the name of the letter once we introduced a second letter or prevented him from rehearsing by, for example, engaging him in conversation.

Finally we returned to one of our earlier assessment techniques and asked him to trace the initial letter with his finger before reading the word. We knew he could do this successfully and that it often led to correct identification. More formal monitoring showed that tracing the letter resulted in a 75% reduction in Ted's error rate. We were thus using an intact (or relatively intact) skill to compensate for an impaired one. Despite our enthusiasm, Ted was not happy with the method because it was slower than visual reading and, as he said, "It's not normal reading." Nevertheless, he resorted to tracing or tactile reading when really challenged by a particular word. This case is described by Patterson and Wilson (1990) and the treatment covered in more detail in Wilson (1999). It is included here to illustrate how a detailed cognitive neuropsychological assessment identified with some precision the nature of Ted's deficit and how a systematic behavioural assessment of several different treatment approaches allowed us to determine the best method to reduce his very specific deficit.

In contrast to Ted's very specific disorder, some patients show extremely widespread deficits in many areas of functioning. One of our most challenging referrals was Meg, a 30-year-old woman who became blind, dysphasic, hemiplegic, and apraxic following an anaesthetic accident. The rehabilitation consultant asked us to determine Meg's level of intellectual functioning. It is not unusual to assess people who cannot speak, or those who are motorically impaired, or those who cannot see, but to be asked to assess a person who is impaired in all these areas is indeed unusual. Traditional neuropsychological tests were obviously inappropriate, so Meg was assessed with developmental checklists designed for children. She performed more poorly than an average 2-year-old on scales of motor, cognitive, and language functioning. Furthermore, her social skills and self-care abilities were no higher than the average 2-year-old. The scales pinpointed particular deficits, such as inability to eat with a spoon, so we were able to successfully target these areas for treatment (Wilson, 1985).

Despite the usefulness of these developmental scales in certain cases, they are limited in their application to people with brain injury as many of the items are inappropriate for adults, so a set of scales for monitoring recovery of functional skills following severe head injury was developed (Shiel, Wilson, McLellan, Horn, & Watson, 2000b). Influenced by Portage (Bluma, Shearer, Frohman, & Hilliard, 1976), and the behavioural observation approach to assessment, the Wessex Head Injury Matrix (WHIM) comprises a 62-item scale to monitor recovery from coma through to emergence from post traumatic amnesia. This is described in more detail later, in Chapter 4.

CONCLUSIONS

This chapter has considered the relative values of neuropsychological and behavioural approaches to assessment: the former identifying cognitive strengths and weaknesses that need to be taken into account when formulating treatment plans; the latter enabling staff to (a) identify problems occurring in everyday life, (b) establish the frequency and severity of these problems, (c) plan rehabilitation or treatment programmes, and (d) monitor the effectiveness of treatment programmes that have been put into operation. Both kinds of assessment are essential in neuropsychological rehabilitation as they provide complementary information that will increase the likelihood of addressing and remediating some of the real problems confronted by people with brain injury in their daily lives.

CHAPTER 3

Planning a rehabilitation programme using a behavioural framework

BACKGROUND

There are numerous treatment techniques for achieving behavioural change. These include methods to increase and decrease behaviours. Systematic desensitisation, flooding, modelling, shaping, and chaining are some of the methods used to teach new skills or increase participation. Positive and negative reinforcement, time out, extinction, response cost, over-correction, and aversive conditioning have all been used to reduce or eliminate undesirable behaviours (see Rimm & Masters, 1979; Wood & McMillan, 2000; Yule & Carr, 1987; for fuller descriptions of these techniques). Wilson (1991a) also provides examples of the use of some of these methods in neuropsychological rehabilitation.

These methods have been applied to numerous problems in many client groups. Not only are behaviour therapy and behaviour modification used with psychiatric clients and people with learning disabilities (the original groups to which these methods were applied), they are also used with people with epilepsy (Lavender, 1981; Melin, Sjödén, & James, 1983), drug addicts (Sobell & Sobell, 1978), and people suffering from hypertension (Johnston & Steptoe, 1989), cardiac problems (Langosch, 1989), irritable bowel syndrome (Thornton, 1989), and diabetes (Fonagy, Moran, & Higgitt, 1989). Since the 1970s behavioural approaches have been used with people with neurological problems including motor problems (e.g., Ince, 1976), emotional problems (e.g., Wilson, 1991a), behaviour disorders (Alderman, 2001), and cognitive problems (Alderman, 2001; Evans, 2001; Wilson, 1992).

The theoretical approaches underlying behaviour therapy and behaviour modification are also diverse. They draw on a number of fields within psychology such as learning theory, information processing, linguistics, developmental psychology, abnormal psychology, and other related disciplines. Because of this there is no one widely accepted definition of behaviour therapy (Kazdin, 1978; Powell, 1981). Kazdin pointed out that features seen by some authors as essential are regarded by others as features that have become outmoded. Eysenck (1959), for example, saw behaviour therapy as relying heavily on experimental psychology, whereas Lazarus (1971) thought that it should draw on *any* discipline that proved to be useful regardless of its particular theoretical orientation. He believed that adherence to any one approach would limit the range of procedures available. Furthermore, many problems faced by practising therapists and their clients would not be informed by research unless the therapists could draw from a wide range of disciplines. This view is close to our own (see Chapter 1) and has been put forward with regard to neuropsychological and cognitive rehabilitation (Wilson, 1997a).

Although it is true that there are differences of opinion as to the nature of behaviour therapy, it is also true that its multifaceted nature is a major strength. The richness and complexity of behavioural approaches mean they can be applied to many areas including neuropsychological rehabilitation. Alderman's work with severely brain-injured people who present with complex behaviour and cognitive problems provides examples of how success can be achieved with a group of people traditionally regarded as difficult to treat (Alderman, Fry, & Youngson, 1995; Alderman & Knight, 1997; Alderman & Ward, 1991).

As we suggested in the foreword, behavioural approaches share common features. Powell (1981) said "all treatments must have a sound theoretical and scientific footing and must not be pure whim on the part of the therapist" (p. 17). Therapists and psychologists should also ensure they monitor and evaluate each treatment to determine (or try to determine) whether any observed change is due to the treatment/intervention strategy or to some non-specific factor such as natural recovery, extra attention, or simple practice. If standardised tests are used to look at change, it is imperative to recognise that some tests have a large practice effect (Gianutsos & Gianutsos, 1987; Wilson, Watson, Baddeley, Emslie, & Evans, 2000b).

SINGLE-CASE VERSUS GROUP DESIGNS

In evaluating the effectiveness of treatment for an individual, single-case designs are usually more helpful than group designs. A typical group study provides different treatments for two or more groups of people, although one group is sometimes subjected to two or more treatments. Usually, results are described in terms of the average or mean response of each group under each condition. Wide individual differences are common. Group studies rarely indicate how many people improve, how many remain unaffected, or how many are made worse by the treatment. The findings are often of little value in predicting whether or not a particular treatment is likely to be effective for a particular person. Because of their quantitative emphasis, group studies highlight statistical significance rather than clinical significance. To illustrate the difference between statistical and clinical significance, consider the following examples. In the field of biofeedback, it might be possible to demonstrate that training a particular muscle in the arm of a stroke patient leads to a statistically significant improvement in the control of that muscle. Clinically or functionally, however, the patient still cannot move the arm or make a cup of tea or get dressed without assistance. Conversely, it might be possible to demonstrate that group training for memory problems is statistically no better than a placebo treatment, but certain individuals within the group may benefit considerably, and their ability to cope with their memory problems may improve.

Single-case experimental designs avoid many of the problems inherent in group studies. The experimenter can tailor the treatment to the individual's particular needs and continuously evaluate his or her responses to the treatment or intervention strategies while controlling for the effects of spontaneous recovery or improvement over time. This is not to deny the value of group studies in some circumstances. Group studies are necessary to answer certain questions, such as how many people are likely to benefit from a given intervention. Wilson (1997a, 1997b) provides a discussion of the benefits of group versus single-case studies.

TYPES OF SINGLE-CASE DESIGNS

The reversal design

The simplest single-case design is the reversal or ABAB design, where A equals baseline and B equals intervention. An example of this design is given by Evans, Emslie, and Wilson (1998) in a programme to help a woman with executive deficits carry out some everyday activities. In the baseline (A) period she frequently forgot to water her plants and to wash her underwear. When reminded to do so with a pager (the treatment or B phase), however, she carried out the activities with 100% success. When the pager was removed (second A phase), she performed just as she had during the first A phase. With the reintroduction of the pager (second B phase), she performed with 100% success, just as before.

Variations on the ABAB design are frequently made. One might, for example, include a C stage in the programme, where C equals an alternative treatment. The design would then become ABAC or ABABC. (For further discussion of these designs, see Hersen & Barlow, 1976; Kazdin, 1982; Kratochwill, 1978.)

Although the reversal design has the benefit of being simple, its application to treatment programmes is limited, for three main reasons. First, it is often impossible to revert to baseline conditions; if a person has been taught to remember the way from the ward to the occupational therapy department, for example, the person cannot "unlearn" this. Second, there are occasions when such an approach is unethical and even dangerous. Suppose, for example, that an amnesic patient has been taught to check whether he or she has left the stove on; then it would be hazardous to revert to a time when the stove was not checked! Third, it is often impracticable to revert to baseline conditions. For instance, when treatment has been successful in preventing a patient from constantly repeating a particular question, then staff and relatives will not welcome a return to the previous state of affairs. Despite these limitations, the reversal design is worth having in one's repertoire of evaluation techniques.

Multiple-baseline designs

Multiple-baseline designs are probably more useful as evaluative procedures, at least as far as cognitive remediation is concerned. There are three main kinds of multiple-baseline design, and each is described in turn.

Multiple-baseline-across-behaviours design. In the multiple-baseline-across-behaviours design, several different behaviours or problems are selected for treatment. Baselines are taken on all the behaviours, but only one is treated at a time. Again, this allows the therapist to separate out the effects of general improvement. An illustration of this design is given by Wilson (1999). A 22-year-old woman who had sustained a very severe head injury remained physically very disabled following 3 months in coma. Physiotherapy exercises were painful and difficult for her. Also, in the past she had received some harsh treatment at another centre shortly after recovering consciousness from the head injury. All these factors would appear to have contributed to her fear. Baselines were taken of the amount of time spent in each of five exercises. One exercise, "head balancing", she actually enjoyed doing—no doubt because it was easy for her. Of the others, three were particularly disliked, and she spent less than 2 minutes on each of these before complaining. A multiple-baseline procedure was used, in which one of the three most disliked exercises was treated each week. The first week after baselines, the patient was (1) asked to try to increase the amount of time spent on that exercise; (2) given verbal feedback on her performance; (3) given visual feedback by means of a graph; and (4) allowed to spend several minutes on the head-balancing exercises if she reached her target (the Premack principle, which means using a liked activity to reinforce a disliked activity.) For the remaining disliked exercises, baselines were still taken, but no encouragement was given. The following week, another disliked exercise was included in the treatment, and in the third week the final exercise was added. Improvement in the amount of time spent on each exercise only occurred after treatment for that exercise was initiated. Thus, the patient's improvement could not be explained by spontaneous recovery or gradual change over time. If this were the case, then all behaviours should have improved at the same time and at the same rate.

Multiple-baseline-across-settings design.   In the multiple-baseline-across-settings design, only one problem or behaviour is tackled, but the effects of treatment are investigated in one setting at a time. This design is useful when situation-specific effects may occur. Carr and Wilson (1983) used this procedure with a spinal patient who forgot (or refused) to lift himself from his wheelchair frequently enough to avoid pressure sores. The patient would not respond to the reasoning or cajoling of physiotherapists, nurses, or doctors. A machine was made that was attached to the wheelchair and recorded the number of lifts made. A lift was defined as the man's buttocks leaving the chair for at least 4 seconds, the patient having pushed himself up with his arms. At least one lift every 10 minutes was considered desirable. Following baselines in four different settings (the workshops, lunchtimes, coffee breaks, and the ward), the machine was fitted to his wheelchair in one setting only (the workshops). Here, the rate of lifting increased dramatically. The next stage was to introduce the machine during lunchtime, then during coffee breaks, and finally on the ward. In each situation, the patient lifted himself the required number of times only *after* the machine had been introduced.

Multiple-baseline-across-subjects design.   Although the multiple-baseline-across-subjects design is not, strictly speaking, a *single*-case design, it is usually included in single-case methodology because the problems with very small groups of subjects are similar to those encountered when $N = 1$. Wilson (1987) used this design in a study that investigated the ability of four men to learn people's names, using a visual-imagery procedure. In the baseline period, patients were asked the names of people at the rehabilitation centre where they were being treated. They were seen individually each day when all the names were tested. However, introduction of treatment was staggered for each individual. Again, improvements only occurred once the treatment procedure was introduced.

Other single-case designs

The three multiple-baseline designs can be applied to a wide range of patients and problems; they are invaluable tools for monitoring intervention strategies. There are other single-case designs. For example, alternating treatments can be used where two or more treatment strategies are employed at the same time (Singh, Beale, & Dawson, 1981). Embedded designs are further variations of the single-case approach, where reversal and multiple-baseline procedures are used together (see, e.g., Wong & Liberman, 1981). Evans (1994) also discusses single-case designs in rehabilitation.

USE OF STATISTICS

Statistics are less often employed in single-case designs than in group studies. There is controversy about their use in single-case studies, with some arguing that if statistics are needed to determine whether or not intervention is effective, then clinical significance is unlikely to have occurred. Others argue that there are occasions when statistics are useful. A supporting example for the latter argument would be the situation in which one is faced by uncontrolled variability in the dependent variable. For further discussion of these arguments, and a description of the statistical techniques appropriate in single-case designs, the reader is referred to Edgington (1982); Evans (1994); Hersen and Barlow (1976); Kazdin (1982); Morley and Adams (1989); Yule and Hemsley (1977).

A BASIC PLAN FOR TREATMENT

The following plan is one we have found useful for a variety of neuropsychological problems. There is a saying that "structure reduces anxiety" and this is true for psychologists and therapists as well as for patients and clients. These steps were probably first used for the management of disruptive behaviours in people with developmental learning difficulties, but we have found them useful for motor problems, emotional problems, reading difficulties, memory problems, and a host of other difficulties faced by people with brain injury.

Step 1

Specify the behaviour to be changed. We need to avoid vague and general descriptions such as "improve concentration" or "reduce memory problems" as it is hard to measure these or to know whether one has made any difference to the behaviour in question. It is better to say, for example, "Fails to use a notebook" or "Asks the same question repeatedly".

Step 2

Decide whether or not an operational definition is needed. Such definitions can be useful for behaviours where it is hard to pin down the problem. For example, poor concentration could be defined (depending on the circumstances) as "unable to stick at a task for more than 3 minutes", or "poor self-control" might mean "throws plates on the floor and shouts at the nurses". Operational definitions usually make it easier to decide what behaviours to measure.

Step 3

State the goals or aims of treatment. Again, these should be clearly specified. For example, the goal for the person with "poor concentration" might be to stick at a task for 15 minutes, three times a day for 5 consecutive days. For the person with "poor self-control" it might be to not throw plates on the floor or shout at the nurses for at least 2 weeks. One could also have goals like "Teach Mr B to check his notebook every half an hour" or determine which of two methods leads to faster learning.

Step 4

Measure the problem (take baselines). This can be achieved in several ways. One can record how frequently the problem occurs (e.g., how many times a question is asked during the course of a therapy session) or how infrequently something happens (e.g., how many times does Mary forget to put on her wheelchair brakes when transferring to the toilet). One could also see how long something takes (e.g., how long does Charlie take to put his sweater on) or measure the output (e.g., how many lines of typing are achieved during a therapy session or how many soiled bibs are placed in the laundry bin during the course of a day). Any of the recording methods described in the behavioural assessment section in Chapter 2 might be appropriate here. The number of baseline sessions required will depend on the frequency and stability of the behaviour, but one should do a minimum of four baselines for a behaviour showing little or no variation over time. For behaviours that show variation over time, one needs to ensure that the baseline is stable. It may also be necessary to carry out a more detailed analysis of other factors such as "does time of day make a difference?" (e.g., unilateral neglect may be worse after physiotherapy or when the person is fatigued); "does the behaviour change when certain people are present/absent?"; "does stress make things worse?"; "does relaxation therapy help?" and so forth.

Step 5

Consider motivators or reinforcers. For many people in neuropsychological rehabilitation success is, in itself, sufficiently motivating, so one does not need to add additional reinforcers. For other people, however, rest, praise, and feedback are probably the most frequently used reinforcers. Even simple feedback such as "yesterday you took 4 minutes to do the task and today you took $3^{1}/_{2}$ minutes" can have a powerful effect. In certain cases, it might be necessary to resort to more tangible reinforcers such as tokens (see Alderman, 2001), extra trips to the hydrotherapy pool, or visits to see some horses (see Wilson, 1999).

Step 6

Plan the treatment. There are several aspects to consider here. Not all will be necessary in every case—the guiding rule is that the plan should be specific enough so that a new member of staff would be able to know how to implement the plan should he or she be required to cover. Possible questions that need to be addressed are:

- *What* strategy/method/procedure should be used?
- *Who* should implement this/do the training?
- *When* and *where* should the training/procedure be carried out?
- *How* should this be carried out—and *how often*?
- *What* happens if the patient/client succeeds? (Is this sufficiently reinforcing, should we say "well done", provide another reinforcer, or what?)
- *What* happens if the patient/client fails? (Should we ignore the failure, prompt the correct response, remind the client of the answer, or what?)
- *How* will success be measured? (It is important to be very specific about success, e.g., "does not repeat the question for at least 30 minutes" or "successfully recalls the word within 30 seconds on three consecutive occasions.)
- *Who* will be responsible for keeping the records? (Will this be everyone in the team, a family member, the patient, an independent observer, or some other?)
- *Who* will be responsible for liaising between the various parties (this might be the case manager, a key worker, a particular therapist, or the psychologist).

Step 7

Begin treatment. This should be easy now that the other steps have been sorted out.

Step 8

Monitor progress—according to the treatment plan outlined in Step 6.

Step 9

Evaluate. Is this going to be done through the record keeping, or through a single-case experimental design, or through a combination of these?

Step 10

Change if necessary. If the programme has succeeded one might consider fading out the cues or prompts, or applying the strategy to another problem. If it has obviously failed then one will probably want to abandon the procedure. If there are some signs of success it might be the case that more time is required, or that the information needs to be presented at a slower rate, or that a combination of two different strategies is necessary.

Step 11

Plan for generalisation. This is a crucial aspect of rehabilitation. Many programmes fail because generalisation has not been included in the treatment plan. Although we can provide people with brain injury with some strategies to overcome their problems or teach them how to cope in a rehabilitation setting, there is no guarantee that strategies or ways of coping learned in rehabilitation will generalise to everyday life. People may use a strategy in one setting such as occupational therapy, for example, but not use it at home. They may use a coping method for one problem but not for another. It is not uncommon to find people who will use a notebook when prompted by the psychologist, but who will not use it spontaneously. Similarly, there are people who can transfer independently in physiotherapy but let relatives help them at home; other people may allow themselves extra time when learning someone's name but not when reading the newspaper. It is important to consider generalisation in every treatment programme.

It is possible to teach generalisation. In developmental learning disability, it is common practice to teach skills in a range of settings to ensure generalisation. This should also happen in neuropsychological rehabilitation. If a patient is taught to use a notebook in occupational therapy, then he/she should also be encouraged (or taught) to use it in other places such as physiotherapy, speech therapy, on the ward, or at home. If someone is taught the names of his/her neighbours in clinical psychology, then it is important to ensure that friends and neighbours are greeted by name in the neighbourhood or in their homes. Relatives can perhaps help with the generalisation here. The important message is that we should not expect generalisation to occur spontaneously. If it does then this is a bonus, but for many and perhaps the majority of people with neuropsychological problems, generalisation should be considered an essential part of the treatment plan.

GOAL PLANNING IN REHABILITATION

Goal planning as a way of organising rehabilitation is becoming increasingly popular. It allows treatment to be targeted to an individual's needs; it avoids the artificial distinction between general outcome measures (such as improvement on standardised test scores or return to work) and client-centred activity; and it makes sense to rehabilitation staff, people with brain injury, and their carers. McMillan and Sparkes (1999) point out that goal planning is not new. It has been used in rehabilitation and other settings for many years with a number of diagnostic groups including people with learning difficulties, spinal injury, cerebral palsy, and brain injury.

Houts and Scott (1975) stated five principles of goal planning: (1) involve the patient, (2) set reasonable goals, (3) describe the patient's behaviour when the goal is reached, (4) set a deadline, and (5) spell out the method so that anyone reading it would know what to do. McMillan and Sparkes (1999) expand on this. They suggest there should be long-term and short-term goals. Long-term goals usually refer to disabilities and handicaps as rehabilitation should improve day-to-day functioning and these goals should be achievable by the time of discharge from the centre. Short-term goals are the steps required to achieve the long-term goals. McMillan and Sparkes (1999) add to the principles of Houts and Scott (1975), saying goals should (a) be client-centred, (b) be realistic and potentially attainable during admission, (c) be clear and specific, (d) have a definite time deadline, and (e) be measurable.

The process of goal-planning approaches typically involves allocation of a chairperson, formulation of a plan of assessment, goal-planning meetings, drawing up a problem list, and plans of action recording whether or not goals are achieved, and if not, why not.

Among the chief advantages of this approach are (1) it makes certain the aims of the admission are clearly documented, (2) patients/clients and relatives/carers are involved, (3) it incorporates a measure of outcomes, and (4) it removes the artificial distinction between outcome and client-centred activity. Among the disadvantages are that it does not provide systematic data on all problems and it is possible to set goals that are too easy. Although sometimes easy goals are set to motivate clients in the early stages of rehabilitation, McMillan and Sparkes (1999) believe this latter point can be resolved with staff training and experience. Our view is that goal planning is one of the most sensible outcome measures, but should not be used for service evaluation because of the shortcomings listed above. Goal planning should always be combined with other more standardised measures such as measures of handicap, mood, psychosocial functioning, and demographics.

Goal planning was used with David, a 41-year-old engineer who had a right hemisphere cerebro-vascular accident in 1998. His main problems, identified by a neuropsychological assessment, were in the areas of (1) attention (visual selective attention, and switching attention from one task to another); (2) executive functions (planning, organising, problem solving, and monitoring behaviour in unstructured situations); (3) memory (specifically when visual attention to fine detail was required); (4) unilateral visual neglect (he tended to ignore stimuli on the left); and (5) mood (he was anxious, lacked confidence, and had low self-esteem).

David attended an intensive, holistic day rehabilitation programme (see Wilson et al., 2000a) where he received both individual and group therapy 5 days a week for 10 weeks and then 1 or 2 days a week for a further few months. These group and individual sessions were designed to (a) increase his understanding of what had happened to him and what his main problems were; (b) enable him to accept that there would be some permanent physical and cognitive changes; (c) teach him strategies and coping methods to reduce his everyday problems; (d) improve his mood; and (e) achieve the goals that had been set through discussions with David, his wife, and the rehabilitation team.

The goals set at the end of a 2-week detailed assessment can be seen in Table 3.1. Each long-term goal is achieved through a series of short-term (ST) goals and action plans. The ST goal specifies what is to be achieved and when;

TABLE 3.1
David's long-term goals

1. David will plan his weekly schedule independently and complete 80% of activities successfully and without reporting excessive fatigue *(through an electronic organiser and written planner)*

2. David will take responsibility for household budgeting and stay within an agreed monthly budget *(through use of a personal organiser and plans with wife)*

3. David will demonstrate effective use of problem-solving strategies in social and functional situations, as rated by himself, his wife Diane, and members of the OZ team *(problem-solving strategies taught in the Problem Solving Group)*

4. David will be engaged in a voluntary work trial and have a personal development plan *(cataloguing books)*

5. David will demonstrate use of strategies to manage his attention difficulties in functional situations *(as rated by self, wife, and OZ team)*

6. David will manage negative automatic thoughts in a range of situations (family/social/leisure) and rate himself as confident in his abilities *(through thought stopping and self-instruction taught in individual sessions and in the Psychological Support Group)*

7. David will report an understanding of the effects of his injury on his personal relationships and identify strategies to manage his relationship more effectively *(through planning ahead with organiser and planner)*

8. David will report an accurate understanding of the consequences of his brain injury *(through attendance at the Understanding Brain Injury Group)*

9. David will engage in a physical leisure activity on a twice-weekly basis *(badminton)*

OZ = Oliver Zangwill Centre for Neuropsychological Rehabilitation

the action plan specifies the process by which the ST goal is to be achieved. The ST goals and action plans set to enable David to achieve his first LT goals can be seen in Table 3.2.

By the time of discharge David had achieved his goals. He was more confident, he had had opportunities to experience and practise successful ways of coping, and he had strategies to enable him to bypass and compensate for his everyday problems. He and his wife reported that David was now reading for pleasure, getting more enjoyment out of watching videos, washing and shaving more efficiently, solving problems more effectively (e.g., sorting out his accommodation and finding lost belongings), and in general was engaged in doing more things.

Other examples of goal planning for people with brain injury can be found in Wilson et al. (2000a) and Wilson, Evans, and Keohane (2002). A special issue of the journal *Neuropsychological Rehabilitation* devoted to "Outcomes in brain injury rehabilitation" (Fleminger & Powell, 1999) contains several articles about goal planning.

The goal-planning approach is very much in the behavioural tradition of specifying what needs to be changed and how to achieve this. We suggest that

TABLE 3.2
Short-term goals set to achieve David's first long-term goal

Long-term goal no. 1: David will plan his weekly schedule independently and complete 80% of activities successfully and without self-reporting excessive fatigue

Date	Short-term goal	Achieved (A), Partly Achieved (P/A), Not achieved (N)	Plans of action
13/8/99	David will identify the strengths and weaknesses of his current scheduling system by 27/8/99	A	David to discuss with Donna method he currently uses to plan his activities and the strengths and weaknesses of this system. David to attend memory group and daily scheduling group
20/8/99	David will demonstrate he can set alarmed reminders and memos on an electronic organiser independently by 3/9/99	A	Sessions with Donna to learn how to use these functions
27/8/99	David to set at least one alarmed reminder per day and complete this task with support by 3/9/99	A	Staff to assist David in daily diary. Donna to monitor overall
1/9/99	David will identify reminders he would need to have on his organiser before leaving his hotel room by 3/9/99	P/A insufficient time with David	Donna to discuss use of electronic organiser in relation to living in accommodation in Ely, e.g., meals, taxis, routines for leaving room. David to use problem-solving framework to select hotel and identify strategies. David to enter alarmed reminders into his organiser
9/9/99	David will demonstrate use of his organiser and attentional strategies to remember to carry out identified tasks whilst in Rehab. flat by 24/9/99	A	David to identify in writing what he needs to remember and how he will do this, then set appropriate reminders on his organiser (with reference to living in hotel accommodation in future). Nita to discuss

goal planning is a sensitive and sensible way to carry out neuropsychological rehabilitation. It is simple, it focuses on practical, everyday problems, it is tailored to the needs of individuals, and includes a measure of outcome, while ensuring that the outcome is tied to real-life functioning. It also involves working alongside the patient and family to ensure cooperation, greater efficiency in the application of behaviour goals, and greater effectiveness in bringing chart improvements in the real-world experience by the patient and his or her family.

CHAPTER 4

Behavioural approaches to assessment and management of people in states of impaired consciousness

INTRODUCTION

Consciousness is a term that can be defined either in strictly medical terms, as in the differentiation between those who are comatose and unresponsive after head injury and those who have "emerged" from coma (Plum & Posner, 1980), or in more philosophical terms, such as references to wakefulness, awareness, knowledge etc. (e.g., Anthony, 1999). Cartlidge (2001) describes consciousness as being characterised by "an awareness of self and environment and an ability to respond to environmental factors" (p. 18). He further defines consciousness as having two components—arousal or wakefulness and awareness of self. However, consciousness is difficult to define in an "all or nothing" context—it is more appropriate to consider it as a continuum rather than a discrete event; that is, patients can progress or deteriorate from one "level" of consciousness to another sometimes. In the more acute stages after brain injury, i.e., during acute coma, this can occur several times a day.

Recovery of consciousness also occurs gradually. People may recover consciousness slowly after brain injury or in some cases consciousness may remain permanently impaired, as with patients in the vegetative state. Observations of people recovering after severe brain injury demonstrate that consciousness may be absent initially, i.e., during the stage of coma, but thereafter may be impaired for a considerable period, i.e., when the patient is in the vegetative state, in the minimally conscious state, or is in post traumatic amnesia (PTA).

Levels of consciousness cannot be assessed directly—an estimate of the level of consciousness is made based on the patient's behavioural responses (or lack of responses) to stimuli. Thus, behavioural change is used routinely with people in states of impaired consciousness to make inferences regarding spontaneous recovery and/or responses to treatment. For example, the Glasgow Coma Scale (Jennett & Teasdale, 1977) records patients' responses to stimuli in terms of motor response, verbal response, and eye opening, and records the response on a hierarchical scale. Based on these responses and behavioural responses to similar measures, people who are recovering from brain injury may be classified as being in coma, in the vegetative state (VS), in the minimally conscious state (MCS) or in post traumatic amnesia (PTA). Patients at any of these stages are in a state of impaired consciousness, and depending on the pattern and rate of recovery, this may persist for some considerable time. In addressing assessment and rehabilitation of people in such states of impaired consciousness, behavioural approaches are employed in two main areas—with regard to assessment and to treatment or management.

States of impaired consciousness after brain injury are defined in two distinct ways—in terms of the behaviours that are absent and in terms of the behaviours that are present. As the descriptions progress through the continuum of recovery it can be noted that there is a shift in emphasis from descriptions of behaviours absent (for example with coma) to those present (for example with PTA). In this chapter each of the states of impaired consciousness is described in behavioural terms. Approaches to assessment and management are then described.

RECOVERY FROM BRAIN INJURY

During recovery after head injury, patients progress through a fairly predictable pattern of recovery. One description of these stages is that of Katz (1992) who described the following "stages" of recovery after diffuse traumatic brain injury.

Stage 1: Coma. The eyes remain closed and there is no sign of responsiveness.
Stage 2: Unresponsive vigilance or vegetative state. Eye opening returns and a sleep–wake cycle commences. There is no sign of responsiveness. Approximately 2% of patients plateau at this stage.
Stage 3: Mute responsiveness. The patient shows signs of responsiveness and may begin to follow commands. Alternatively, some patients' verbal abilities may return before commands are followed.
Stage 4: Confusional state. Some cognitive and communicative functions recover but there are severe memory and attentional deficits and capacity to learn is reduced. This is the stage of post traumatic amnesia (PTA).
Stage 5: Independence. The patient emerges from PTA and is capable of more interaction. Cognitive functions such as mental speed and efficiency and abstract reasoning may still be impaired and behaviour problems may be evident.

Apart from the fifth stage described, patients recovering from a brain injury can be classified as being in a state of impaired consciousness during each of these stages. However, patients do not pass automatically from one stage to the next—they may cease to progress at any stage after the end of coma or may plateau at any of these stages. Approaches to assessment and rehabilitation therefore need to reflect this. In what follows, the relevant stages (i.e., those where the patient can be described as being in a state of impaired consciousness) are described behaviourally with descriptions of the behaviours that are specific to some stages and those that are common to more than one stage.

COMA

Descriptions of coma are numerous and there are a variety of definitions. However, although the definitions vary, the behavioural features of coma remain constant and include the following:

- No arousal and no awareness
- No eye opening
- Reflex movements only
- No language comprehension
- No purposeful response

The most widely used and accepted definition of coma is that of Jennett and Teasdale (1977) who describe a patient in coma as "giving no verbal response, not obeying commands and not opening the eyes spontaneously or to stimulation" (p. 878). However, while these features are present in coma, all but lack of eye opening are also characteristic of the vegetative state. Traumatic coma *per se* is short-lived and within 2–4 weeks the patient will have progressed either to being "awake" or, if the patient continues to be unresponsive, to the vegetative state.

THE VEGETATIVE STATE

The vegetative state is the description most commonly used to describe the state of complete unresponsiveness observed where the patient is not in coma—i.e., eye opening is present. There are numerous descriptions of the syndrome and a variety of terms with their own definitions and descriptions have been proposed, but essentially all describe the same phenomenon. Jennett and Plum (1972) coined the term "persistent vegetative state" but the term of choice in the UK and the USA at present is either "vegetative state" or "chronic vegetative state". This is because the term "persistent" implies that there will be no change. While this is undoubtedly true for the majority of patients who are vegetative after a significant period of time, a small minority may recover to some extent. Berrol (1990) described the features of the vegetative state as follows:

- Spontaneous eye opening
- Sleep–wake cycles
- Spontaneous maintenance of blood pressure
- Regular respiratory pattern
- No localisation to pain
- No vocalisation
- No response to commands
- Lack of sustained visual pursuit

Two more recent reports on the vegetative state (VS) are those produced by the Royal College of Physicians (RCP) (1996) and by Andrews, Murphy, Munday, and Littlewood (1996). The report by the RCP states three criteria which must be met if a patient is to be diagnosed as being in VS: first, that patients show no evidence of awareness, no volitional response, and no evidence of language comprehension; second, that a cycle of eye opening and closure is present; and third, that hypothalamic and brain stem function is intact. Further behavioural features, which may also be observed in patients in the vegetative state, include incontinence, spontaneous blinking, occasional movements of eyes or head, aimless movement of limbs or trunk, and facial grimacing. Such movements are referred to as "purposeless" or "reflexive" although the basis on which judgements are made is not always explicit. In contrast to this clinical description of the syndrome, Andrews et al. (1996) acknowledged the difficulties of diagnosis of the vegetative state, and suggested that behavioural description of patients rather than distinguishing between coma, vegetative presentation, and an "undecided" category, which may include profound brain damage and borderline or transitional states, is more appropriate. Andrews et al. recommended that the most appropriate method of assessment would be to describe the level of responsiveness in behavioural terms and to describe but not to interpret any movements or behaviours observed.

THE MINIMALLY CONSCIOUS STATE

In recent years a new category of responsiveness, that of "the minimally conscious state", has been recognised. This term has been coined to distinguish between those who can no longer be described as being in the vegetative state but whose behavioural repertoire is very severely compromised.

Distinguishing between those who are vegetative and those who could be described as "minimally conscious" is not easy. Misdiagnosis appears to be common. Childs, Mercer, and Childs (1993), in a study of patients in the vegetative state, found that diagnosis was incorrect in 37% of cases—in other words, more than one third of the patients described as being in the vegetative state were not. More recently, Andrews et al. (1996) reported similar findings with patients admitted to their unit. While these studies raise serious concerns about the accuracy of diagnosis with this patient group, for the majority of patients a change in diagnosis from "vegetative" to "minimally conscious" does not imply any useful functional gain or change in prognosis but may have enormous implications for the injured person's family and for whether rehabilitation is offered.

While the recent development of criteria regarding the vegetative state has clarified differences between vegetative and minimally conscious patients, the parameters of the minimally conscious state are not yet clear. Although it is possible to distinguish between coma, VS, and the minimally conscious state with some degree of confidence, it is less easy to decide whether minimally responsive patients can or should be distinguished from patients with severe disability.

Rosenberg and Ashwal (1996) suggested the following distinctions between patients who are in coma, vegetative, or minimally responsive. Patients in *coma* have no self-awareness, are not aware of pain, do not have sleep–wake cycles or purposeful movement, and may have depressed respiratory functions. Coma evolves over a 2–4 week period into consciousness, the vegetative state, or death. Patients in the *vegetative state* have no self-awareness, do not feel pain, have sleep–wake cycles, have no purposeful movement, and normal respiratory function. *Minimally responsive* patients have limited self-awareness and do feel pain. They may also have sleep–wake cycles and severely limited movement. Respiratory function may be depressed. Leaving the issue of whether patients in coma can feel pain aside, these distinctions are clear.

ASSESSMENT

During the time that the patient is in a state of impaired consciousness, any behaviours observed are likely to occur at unpredictable and infrequent intervals. While rehabilitation during this period is, of necessity, concentrated on avoiding further complications, e.g., contractures, accurate assessment is essential to identify realistic short-term goals. Regular assessment of head-injured patients beginning as soon as possible after traumatic brain injury is essential to clarify the behavioural indications of recovery and response to rehabilitation. Such observations may give an indication of the sequences of recovery of different skills and may be useful in suggesting optimum timing of different interventions. They may also give the opportunity to evaluate the success of different learning approaches, allowing these to be adjusted, both to optimise the patient's learning ability and to respond to biological change.

Examples of scales designed to assess patients in coma or emerging from coma include the Glasgow Coma Scale (GCS) (Teasdale & Jennett, 1974); the Disability Rating Scale (Rappaport, Hall, Hopkins, Belleza, & Cope, 1982); the Rancho Los Amigos Scale (Hagen, Malkmus, & Durham, 1987); and the Neurobehavioural Rating Scale (Levin et al., 1987). More recently, developments have concentrated on expansion of currently available scales, e.g., the expansion of the Glasgow Coma Scale to the Coma/Near Coma Scale (Rappaport, Dougherty, & Kelting, 1992). However, many of these scales are not widely used and have been criticised by Horn et al. (1993) because:

(1) The majority are rating scales—that is to say, the patient's behaviour is rated by the assessor in response to a stimulus. This means that the assessor has to make a judgement as to the "purposefulness" of the response. This is problematic in that the same behaviour may represent a purposeful response in one individual and a random behaviour in another—or the same may be true in one individual on different occasions.
(2) Most scales are multidimensional; they cross a variety of behavioural dimensions, e.g., cognitive functions, motor skills, and so on. This means that in some cases, proof of cognitive recovery is dependent on physical ability, e.g., ability to point to, reach towards, or manipulate.
(3) Most scales have ordinal scoring, i.e., a behavioural description such as response to pain may be scored as 2 for extension and 3 for flexion. The difficulty arises where these scores are summed, often across dimensions, to produce a total score. As the numbers are not absolute numbers and a variety of dimensions are grouped together, this means that it is unclear whether all functions are improving at the same rate or whether some are changing more quickly than others.

In order to identify progress or deterioration and to set appropriate goals, it is essential to use a sensitive and practical measure. An example of such a measure which has recently been developed is the Wessex Head Injury Matrix (WHIM) (Shiel et al., 2000a, 2000b). The WHIM was developed as a behavioural assessment to monitor recovery and response to rehabilitation after severe brain injury. Kazdin (1980) defines behavioural assessment as "direct measurement of the behaviours of interest" (p. 234) and comments further that the aim of a behavioural assessment is to establish what the patient can actually do. If the aim of assessment is to establish the routine level of performance rather than the capacity for performance, behavioural assessment is a method whereby this can be achieved. While it is equally important to establish the level of capacity in order to set realistic goals, level of performance may be less frequently assessed in rehabilitation, as the cueing and structure that is provided in many standard tests may mean that patients perform at a higher level than they would in a less structured environment. A further important feature of behavioural assessments is that the measures used can be developed specifically to meet the needs of each individual. However, Kazdin (1980) also warns of the risk of unreliability and bias in using such techniques and recommends strongly that all behaviours being assessed are operationally defined. However, as long as the behaviours being assessed are defined explicitly, behavioural assessment can be a powerful tool in examining a complex issue such as recovery after severe traumatic brain injury.

The WHIM was developed in response to a need for such an assessment identified by Wilson (1988). The aim was to develop an assessment technique in which data could be collected by observation and by testing tasks used in everyday life. This approach was appropriate for use with head-injured patients at all stages of recovery because it addressed a range of abilities of real-life skills, was administered by observation, and was therefore acceptable and unobtrusive for use with head-injured patients. The operational basis for the development of the WHIM came from the clinical approach to the description of behaviours commonly used in brain injury rehabilitation. The intention was to establish which behaviours patients with head injury were observed to show and construct this into a measure that met the specific needs of individual patients, in order to bridge the gap between those scales that are useful in the very acute stages after head injury such as the Glasgow Coma Scale (GCS), and standard tests of cognition, motor skills, and dependency which cannot be applied until the later stages of recovery.

The result is a scale that effectively divides clinical recovery from the time of injury into small steps which can be used to evaluate progress from the point of admission to emergence from PTA. It includes items of communication, social behaviour, cognition, attention, and communication. Although all the behaviours require the ability to make some kind of response, unlike other scales no assumption as to the purpose of the response or the level of awareness is made. The responses are recorded but are not rated or evaluated. The items on the scale are assessed by observation and by documenting the patient's response to a set of standard stimuli, and items are fine-grained enough to show small increments. The items on the scale also have the potential to be used to formulate short-term goals for rehabilitation. The WHIM is administered regularly—if patients are changing rapidly it is administered daily; for patients who do not change for more than 3 days it is administered twice weekly; for patients who do not change for a week it is administered weekly; and for patients who do not change for a month it is administered monthly. If rate of change alters, the assessment schedule is revised as appropriate.

Another recently developed scale which is specifically designed for use with people considered to be in the vegetative state is the Sensory Modality Assessment and Rehabilitation Technique (SMART) (Gill-Thwaites & Munday, 1999). The SMART records patients' responses to sensory and environmental stimulation and evaluates these in a 5-point hierarchy from no response to a consistent purposeful response. It is used as an assessment tool and a treatment tool simultaneously, and depending on scores, patients are classified as being vegetative or minimally conscious. For assessment purposes, the SMART is administered on a regular basis, and uses structured stimulation of each of the senses and evaluates the response. For treatment purposes the same technique and stimuli are used.

The WHIM and the SMART present a new approach to assessment of brain-injured people. The scales are compatible in that the WHIM is appropriate for use at all stages after brain injury once the patient's eyes are open, and has a higher ceiling, i.e., it is used with patients until they have emerged from post traumatic amnesia. The SMART is designed for a specific patient group, and has a lower floor, i.e., it is appropriate for use with patients who show no evidence of anything other than reflex responses either spontaneously or to stimulation. Thus, patients who have reached ceiling on the SMART can be assessed using the WHIM, and patients below the floor of the WHIM can be assessed using the SMART.

CASE EXAMPLES

Coma

BR, a 22-year-old man, had a head injury after a fall which happened after a night out at a party. He was found unconscious at the foot of the stairs the following morning. On admission to A&E his GCS was 3 (E1, V1, M1) and after resuscitation this improved to 4 (E1, V1, M2). CT scan showed a large temporo-parietal subdural haematoma with midline shift and brain swelling. Following neurosurgical removal of the haematoma, he was sedated, paralysed, and ventilated. On withdrawal of sedation and paralysing drugs 1 week later, he breathed spontaneously, but his GCS remained unchanged at 4. By the next week his GCS had stabilised and was now 8 at best (M3, E4, V1). He was no longer in coma, was not obeying commands or verbalising, but his eyes were open. Although his GCS remained unchanged for the next few weeks, assessment on the WHIM showed slow but steady progress with visual tracking, eye contact, and selective responses to specific individuals all improving gradually (see Figure 4.1). This information facilitated setting of realistic and appropriate goals such as increasing visual tracking from 1–2 seconds to 5 seconds, tracking sounds, and maintaining eye contact for 5 seconds or more. All of these goals were addressed by the rehabilitation team and were encouraged during nursing care, physiotherapy, and occupational therapy as well as by the patient's family.

BR continued to make steady progress over the following months and as his level of function improved, assessment on functional scales and neuropsychological tests commenced and more demanding goals were set as appropriate. However, use of the WHIM facilitated starting his rehabilitation programme while he was still in the intensive care environment, and provided an appropriate and sensitive measure of subtle changes in the earliest stage of recovery.

Vegetative or minimally conscious?

FC, an 80-year-old man, was knocked down by a car on his way to a meeting and was admitted to a regional neurosurgical unit. Prior to the accident he had been fit and healthy and had led an active life. He had no *known* significant medical history. On admission to the neurosurgical unit, his GCS was 3 and an

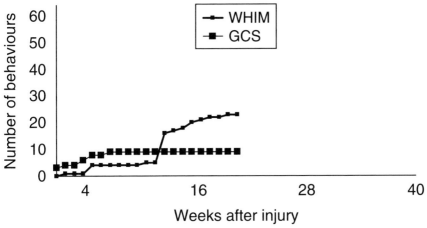

FIG. 4.1   GCS and WHIM in early recovery.

initial CT scan showed multiple focal haemorrhages with evidence of a small old right parietal infarct (which had apparently caused no impairments or disabilities). He was treated conservatively and his GCS increased to 6 over the next month. He had a tracheostomy and was unable to speak. He was denied rehabilitation because of his age and "lack of rehabilitation potential" and was admitted to a continuing care unit with a diagnosis of being in the vegetative state. By now (6 months after injury) he had severe contractures in his left arm (fingers, wrist, and elbow) and left leg (hip, knee, and ankle). He also had a pelvic windswept deformity. He was cared for in bed and spent most of the day lying flat facing a wall with his eyes closed.

FC was referred to the occupational therapy department at the continuing care unit. Standard functional and neuropsychological assessments were inappropriate at this stage, so assessment was commenced using the WHIM. Initial assessment suggested that he was unresponsive, as he remained motionless and kept his eyes closed. However, when his eyes were opened passively, he immediately made eye contact and tracked through 180°. It was decided to carry out a structured programme programme of assessment and stimulation to establish his level of cognitive function and the following goals were set:

• To establish FC's level of cognitive function.
• To alter the environment to make it more interesting.
• To assess for and provide a suitable seating system so F could leave the ward and use the garden, and could be brought from the ward to the OT and PT departments.
• To change staff attitudes—up to this point staff only spoke to FC when carrying out care. Therefore his tone increased dramatically each time he was approached

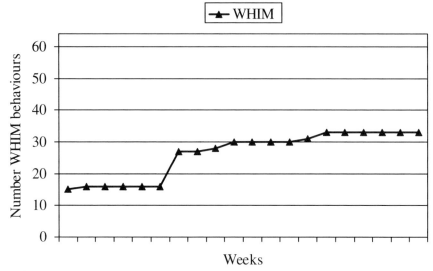

FIG. 4.2   Response to rehabilitation in a patient diagnosed as being in the vegetative state.

by a member of staff. Staff were asked to stop and speak to FC whenever possible, and if they had a few minutes to spare to orient him to where he was and why, and day, date, and time of day.

Over a period of a few months FC's level of cognitive function was assessed daily and then weekly on the WHIM. The change in scores is shown in Figure 4.2. He quickly became consistent in obeying commands and became much more responsive both to staff and to his family. He was assessed for a wheelchair and when this was supplied he was seated out of bed daily.

During the following months his arousal levels increased until he had his eyes open for most of the day. He developed a consistent "yes" and "no" response to questions. He showed a selective response to his family and after some time to those members of staff he worked with most. He attended OT on a regular basis and enjoyed using a computer and looking at Internet sites related to areas he was interested in before his accident. When he was presented with written materials he scanned pages from left to right and appeared to be reading the text. Several months after the referral he became ill (from an unrelated condition) and died.

While this patient was severely disabled with a compromised behavioural repertoire, assessment on the WHIM showed clearly that he was not in a vegetative state. Indeed, it could be questioned whether he was ever in a vegetative state, as his arousal level was such that initially at any rate, the assessor had to be forceful in order to get a response. Accurate assessment using the WHIM facilitated identification of appropriate and achievable goals and resulted in a greatly enhanced environment for both the patient and his family.

POST TRAUMATIC AMNESIA

Post traumatic amnesia (PTA) occurs during the period after which the patient emerges from coma. There are numerous definitions of PTA, ranging from that of Russell and Nathan (1946) who described it as the time up to which the patient can give a clear and concise account of what is happening. Wilson et al. (1999) comment that the use of the term amnesia is ambiguous, in that it implies that the major deficit is one of memory, whereas recent research with people in PTA has demonstrated clearly that a number of cognitive functions are impaired during this stage (Wilson, Baddeley, Shiel, & Patton, 1992; Wilson et al., 1999).

The most striking features of PTA are disorientation, loss of memory, poor attention, distractibility, and slowed reaction time. Patients in PTA may also be hypersomnic, emotionally labile, agitated, and occasionally aggressive. As they may be fully mobile and able to speak and respond appropriately to some questions, it would be easy to conclude that the level of consciousness is no longer impaired. However, if they are observed more closely, it becomes clear that although arousal may be within normal limits, awareness is not. During this time there may be brief "islands" when the patient appears to be oriented and retaining information, and this may be a sign that the patient is beginning to emerge from PTA. Such fluctuations may continue for a long time and are deceptive if the patient is in an island of awareness during assessment.

In comparison to patients who are in coma, in the vegetative state, or who are minimally conscious, patients in PTA may be perceived as being difficult to manage in the ward environment. Behaviours that may be observed include restlessness, agitation, anxiety, difficulty understanding and following instructions, poor attention, and in some cases verbal and physical aggression. Alternatively, patients may present as being extremely passive and adynamic. Regardless of which type of behaviour is presented, it should be remembered that these behaviours are not "purposeful" and occur as a result of impaired awareness, confusion, fear, and disorientation. For example, a patient may be unable to understand why he or she is in hospital, and this may result in wandering particularly at night. A behaviour such as aggression may thus be the result of being upset when prevented from wandering, e.g., when the patient wants to leave the ward.

Assessment of patients in PTA

Given the range of deficits demonstrated by patients in PTA, it is clear why the question of assessment of and during PTA is problematic. The range of impairments shown by patients is huge; yet the patients have very poor attention during this stage and are unable to participate in formal testing for anything other than a very short period. This creates problems in establishing with a great deal of reliability when exactly the patient emerged from PTA, thereby the duration of PTA, and perhaps an indication of the severity of the brain injury.

There are two types of PTA assessment used—prospective and retrospective. Prospective assessments refer to ongoing assessment on a daily or weekly basis when the patient is in hospital. Retrospective assessments refer to assessments carried out "after the event", i.e., later in the recovery process.

Retrospective assessments are usually done by interview and the typical approach is to ask the patient when he or she remembers waking up. However, this may give a falsely short indication of the duration of PTA as the patient may report an island of memory. Reliability of retrospective assessment may be improved by using a semi-structured interview with both the family and the patient and then comparing accounts. Close questioning regarding actual events recalled by the patient is also useful if these can be verified. However, another difficulty with retrospective assessment is that although patients may appear to recall events, answers may reflect the fact that families have been relating events that occurred to the patient, who does not have a true memory of the event. However, retrospective assessment can be useful, as the duration of PTA is not often recorded prospectively.

Prospective assessment of PTA refers to regular assessment of functions related to PTA status while the patient is in or emerging from PTA. There are two possible methods—careful questioning and interviewing, including questions to assess the degree of orientation and day-to-day memory function, and/or use of standardised tests. A number of standardised tests have been produced. One thing all have in common, however, is that they are quite old. They were developed well before the recent work examining the range of functions affected was carried out. Therefore one of the main features of the assessments is that they assess PTA by examining patients' performance on tests of memory and orientation.

Levin, O'Donnell, and Grossman designed the Galveston Orientation and Amnesia Test (GOAT) in 1979. It is widely used in the USA but not in the UK. It consists of questions of biographical information including name, address, and date of birth, orientation including time and place, recall of events prior to and surrounding the accident, and a description of the first memory after the accident. The test should be administered at least once daily. However criticisms levelled at the GOAT include the fact that recovery of orientation does not necessarily mean that the person is out of PTA, and that patients can achieve a "normal" score on the test even while failing all of the memory questions.

The Westmead scale is an extension of a scale developed by I Fortuny, Briggs, Newcombe, Ratcliffe, and Thomas (1980). In this test the patient is asked to give their age, date of birth, place, and time, they are asked to remember the examiner's face, and are asked to remember pictures of three common objects. If they do not know the answer they are given a forced choice, i.e., is it X or Y. A total score of 12 is possible and when patients score a maximum score on three separate occasions they are considered to be out of PTA from the first occasion.

BEHAVIOURAL APPROACHES TO TREATMENT: COMA, VEGETATIVE STATE, AND MINIMAL CONSCIOUSNESS

There is little literature on specific rehabilitation interventions for patients in PTA. Rehabilitation during the early stage of recovery, i.e., coma, may concentrate on avoiding further complications such as contractures, but accurate assessment is essential to identify realistic and achievable short-term rehabilitation goals. An example of a realistic short-term goal could be extending the length of eye opening once this has begun to occur. While this may be a function of the level of arousal, timely assessment may reveal the patient's optimum capacity. For example a joint assessment with physiotherapists (when arousal is likely to be at its highest) may reveal behaviours not demonstrated when the patient is observed lying in bed. The same is true for those patients who could be described as vegetative or minimally conscious. For these patients, examples of realistic goals could include pre-communicative and social behaviours such as "looking at a person briefly" or "making eye contact".

Rehabilitation of the patient in a state of impaired consciousness differs from that of other groups of patients, in that the patients cannot participate in any way in goal setting. As goals that appear relevant to both the patient and family are more likely to be acceptable, it is essential to have input from families as to the patient's likes and dislikes, lifestyle, and interests in so far as this is possible. This information can be incorporated into treatment programmes—for example by using a favourite piece of music as a reinforcer. It is also important to establish from an early stage what expectations the family have of rehabilitation and to make clear the need to set realistic and achievable goals. If the goals set are realistic and achievable, some are more likely to be achieved, thereby maintaining both staff and family motivation. Methods of intervention used at this stage should also vary and include stimuli that the patient is likely to respond to. Examples of such stimuli have been reported previously (Watson & Horn, 1991).

Treatment approaches with patients in states of impaired consciousness are also limited. While it is desirable at all times to carry out rehabilitation with the patient in certain circumstances (e.g., coma and the vegetative state in particular) it may be necessary to give treatment to the patient. It is also worth bearing in mind that patients in impaired states of consciousness are likely to fatigue very quickly. Treating in a quiet environment may help this but most patients can tolerate only minutes of treatment in the earlier stages of recovery before becoming unresponsive.

BEHAVIOURAL APPROACHES TO
TREATMENT: PTA

Although patients who are in PTA can interact more fully than those patients described above, rehabilitative approaches still have to take account of the fact that their consciousness is not only impaired but also fluctuates throughout the day. Behavioural approaches may be used in a variety of ways with patients who have reached this stage of recovery. Examples can include behavioural analysis (e.g., ABC to establish whether specific stimuli correspond to specific behaviours), modification of the environment, and modification of therapeutic approaches (Martin, 1991). ABC refers to antecedent—behaviour—consequence. This is an observational protocol where the behaviour of interest is observed from the perspective of the events or behaviours immediately preceding the behaviour (antecedent) and the result of the behaviour (consequence). For example, patients in PTA are frequently cared for in a single side-room on a ward. Table 4.1 shows an example of part of an ABC chart for such a patient. He was being cared for in a side-room but was described by ward staff as being constantly abusive and spending all day screaming and shouting.

Evaluation of the information in Table 4.1 shows that there is a common antecedent factor. The patient is always alone when he shouts and screams. A more detailed set of observations showed that when J was quiet, staff seldom if ever entered the room. The belief on the ward was that "if there's a problem, he'll let us know". The difficulty was addressed by asking staff to alter their behaviour. Instead of only entering the room when J was shouting, they made an effort to go in when he was quiet. When he screamed, staff were asked to check that he was all right but not to speak to him or delay at all. Finally, his bed was turned so he could see through the door, and staff were asked to speak to him as

TABLE 4.1
Part of Patient J's ABC chart

Antecedent	Behaviour	Consequence
J alone in room. TV on, bed faced towards window, away from door	Screaming and shouting—no identifiable words	Member of staff comes into room and asks why J is shouting. J silent
		Checks he doesn't need to be changed and that feed is operating correctly and leaves
Member of staff leaves. J alone in room again. TV on, bed faced towards window, away from door	Screaming and swearing	Member of staff returns, reprimands J for his language, tells him there is nothing to shout about and leaves
		J moans for 30 seconds and then recommences screaming

they passed. The programme was successful in that although the screaming did not cease, it was much less frequent.

Patients in PTA cannot participate in several aspects of rehabilitation—for example in setting goals. Furthermore, the degree of cognitive deficit means that therapeutic approaches must be carefully considered to minimise distress and to maximise effectiveness. Patients may respond poorly to overstimulation, so control of the environment both in therapy/assessment sessions and on the ward is likely to facilitate optimum cooperation. A number of simple measures may be considered to achieve this. Examples include nursing the patient in a single room or a small room (rather than a large ward) if possible, reducing noise where possible (for example not leaving radio/TV/music playing continuously), and limiting the number of visitors at a time and the duration of the visits. Such measures will also help to prevent over-fatigue, which in some cases can result in verbal and/or physical aggression. Although physical aggression is a major problem when it does occur, it is best managed by environmental means within the constraints of the ward wherever possible. Behavioural analysis can assist in identifying triggers for such behaviour and thereby the means of dealing with it. For example, a patient who is allowed to wander rather than being constantly turned back is less likely to be aggressive. Frequently this can be achieved by going in a circle (i.e., going straight on rather than trying to get the patient to turn back) rather than insisting the patient returns. Other examples of environmental manipulation may include having some of the patient's personal possessions in the ward/room to give a feeling of familiarity.

During the stage of PTA, short but frequent therapy sessions are likely to be most effective, as patients cannot attend for long sessions and thus cannot participate in therapy sessions for long periods. If over-arousal causes problems with behaviour it may be appropriate to limit the number of visitors. Frequent rest periods are also helpful in ensuring maximum participation during therapy.

Case example

EG was involved in a road traffic accident in which he sustained severe head injuries and also severe orthopaedic injuries. He had a fractured pelvis, femur, ribs, and clavicle. Initially he remained unresponsive when sedation was withdrawn but in the following week he rapidly regained consciousness. At this stage he was cared for in a side-room of an orthopaedic ward and was confined to bed because he had to remain non-weight-bearing on his fractured bones. As his level of arousal rose he constantly tried to get out of bed and climbed over the cot-sides onto a bedside locker on more than one occasion. In an attempt to manage the situation, ward staff placed a sign by his bed explaining that he had fractures and had to remain in bed, but this was unsuccessful as the patient forgot the note was there, and even when he did see it he did not remember the contents. Behavioural observation by naturalistic observation and assessment using the WHIM showed that the patient had dense memory impairment and severe attentional deficits such that he retained information for less than 5 minutes. The situation was dealt with by modifying the patient's environment. First he was moved from the single room to a four-bedded ward opposite the nurses' station. This had a double advantage—first, when the nursing staff were at the desk they were able to remind him to stay in bed when they saw him beginning to move, and second, the other patients in the ward (who were not head-injured) also reminded him to stay in bed or called the nurses when he tried to get up.

This solution worked well for the next 2 weeks until EG emerged from PTA. However it is a short-term solution to a short-term problem. Had EG's dense memory impairment persisted, more permanent alternative solutions would have had to be found.

CONCLUSION

Behavioural approaches are invaluable tools in the assessment and management of patients in reduced states of awareness. The advantages of using such approaches include the fact that assessment is of performance rather than capacity, i.e., what the patient *does* do rather than what the patient *can* do. This is an advantage, as one of the difficulties encountered in assessing head-injured patients is the mismatch between capacity and performance. While it is also important to assess capacity, in order to make rehabilitation and discharge goals more realistic assessment of performance is more important. Observations and data collection can be carried out in a variety of settings and situations. Head-injured patients may be cared for in a variety of settings, e.g., specialist neurological, intensive therapy, acute orthopaedic, or rehabilitation units in the acute recovery phase. Behavioural assessments can be carried out in all of these settings, ensuring continuity of data collection. The incidence, intensity, and frequency of behaviour can be recorded, and variation in behaviour related to timing or environment can be identified.

However it should be remembered that there may also be some disadvantages to behavioural approaches. These could include the fact that the behaviours observed in an individual on a single occasion may not be representative of the range of behaviours either for that individual or for the client group as a whole. Behavioural observation can be a costly and time-consuming exercise, particularly if the target behaviours are low-frequency and occur at (apparently) random intervals so that variations in intensity or frequency of behaviour may not be evident.

It is not suggested that behavioural methods are the only approach to assessment and management of patients in reduced states of consciousness. They are, however, a very useful tool for assessing, treating, and managing a patient group where the complexity of the impairments may limit the usefulness of other approaches.

CHAPTER 5

Behavioural approaches to the remediation of cognitive deficits

Behavioural approaches are frequently incorporated into cognitive rehabilitation programmes because they provide a structure, a way of analysing cognitive problems, a means of assessing everyday manifestations of cognitive problems, and a means of evaluating the efficacy of treatment. In addition, behavioural approaches supply us with a number of strategies including shaping, chaining, modelling, desensitisation, flooding, extinction, positive reinforcement, response cost, and so on, all of which can be modified or adapted to suit particular cognitive problems.

Behaviour therapy and behaviour modification are concerned both with establishing or improving appropriate behaviours and with the decrease or elimination of inappropriate behaviours. Cognitive rehabilitation can be defined as a process whereby brain-injured people work together with health professionals and others to remediate or alleviate cognitive deficits arising from a neurological insult (Wilson, 1996, p. 488). The process of cognitive rehabilitation includes establishing or improving appropriate behaviours (for example, teaching people to compensate for memory deficits or to apply problem-solving strategies in real-life situations). It is also concerned with reducing inappropriate behaviours that might impact on cognition (for example, reducing anxiety that may further impair damaged memory skills or eliminating perseverative behaviour in someone with frontal lobe damage). Thus, there is no inherent conflict between cognitive rehabilitation and behavioural treatments. Indeed, as pointed out in Chapter 1, the two have been partners for many years.

BEHAVIOURAL APPROACHES FOR INCREASING OR ESTABLISHING COGNITIVE FUNCTIONING

In developmental learning disability there is a belief that it is easier to teach people to do something than it is to teach them not to do something. We are not sure whether this is true in cognitive rehabilitation. For example, is it easier to teach someone to use a memory aid than it is to teach them not to worry about memory failures? It is certainly true that both are possible and that they are, at times, two sides of the same coin. Thus, if we teach people to compensate for their memory deficits we are also teaching them not to make so many everyday memory failures, which, in turn, means they may worry less.

Strategies that have proved useful in teaching new skills or improving existing skills include prompting, chaining, shaping, expanding rehearsal, positive reinforcement, and goal planning. Prompting was used to teach self-care skills to Sarah, a young woman with severe anoxic brain damage following an anaesthetic accident (Wilson, 1999). The young woman appeared to have apraxia and Balint's syndrome, in that she had difficulty sequencing her movements despite the fact that she had no muscle weakness or paralysis and she was unable to localise objects in space. This meant she was completely dependent on others for feeding, washing, dressing, and all other self-care skills. Following an assessment, which included the Portage developmental checklists (Bluma et al., 1976) and the Vineland Social Maturity Scale (Doll, 1953), it was established that (a) she failed a number of tasks most children of 1 or 2 years old could do, (b) she had the appropriate physical strength to carry out these tasks, and (c) she understood what was required of her. One of her first failures on the Portage and Vineland was failure to drink from a cup alone, consequently this was selected as the first goal for treatment. A series of prompts was used to teach her to drink unaided. The task was broken down into a number of steps written as directions:

1. Put your hand flat on the table
2. Keep your hand low
3. Put your thumb through the handle of the cup
4. Grasp the handle
5. Lift the cup to your mouth
6. Drink
7. Put the cup down on the table
8. Open your fingers
9. Release your fingers and take your thumb out of the handle.

As Sarah tended to put the further rim of the cup to her mouth causing spillage, it was decided, after the seventh teaching session, to add another step between steps 5 and 6. This asked her to look for the red rim painted on the side of the cup that was nearer to her mouth.

TABLE 5.1
Teaching Sarah to drink from a cup

Day	Session	Steps								
		1	*2*	*3*	*4*	*5*	*6*	*7*	*8*	*9*
1	1	4	4	4	4	4	1	3	2	2
	2	2	2	2	2	1	1	2	2	2
	3	1	1	1	1	1	1	1	1	1
2	4	2	2	2	2	1	1	1	1	1
3	5	1	1	2	3	4	1	1	1	1
	6	1	2	2	4	4	1	1	1	1
	7	1	2	2	1	1*	1	1	2	1
4	8	1	2	1	3	4	1	2	1	1
	9	1	2	1	2	2	1	1	1	1
	10	1	2	1	2	2	1	1	1	1
	11	2	2	2	2	1	1	2	1	1
5	12	2	1	3	2	2	1	1	1	1
6	13	1	1	1	1	1	1	1	1	1
7	14	1	1	1	1	1	1	1	1	1
8	15	1	1	1	1	1	1	1	1	1

1 = no prompt; 2 = verbal prompt; 3 = mild physical prompt; 4 = full physical prompt/guidance.

Breaking the task down like this looks like a chaining procedure, but in Sarah's case the steps were not taught one at a time. Instead, she was required to complete all steps by herself. A scoring procedure was devised whereby if Sarah completed a step without help she was awarded 1 point. If she was unable to do this, or made a wrong movement, a verbal prompt was given. If she succeeded with the verbal prompt she scored 2 points. If that failed she was given a slight physical prompt (in the form of a nudge in the right direction). This scored 3 points and, if all else failed, a full physical prompt was supplied (i.e., her hand was guided through the step). If this last form of prompt was given, Sarah scored 4 points. Results of this programme can be seen in Table 5.1.

This programme was initiated a year after Sarah's accident. It is very unlikely that spontaneous recovery caused her success, given that she had previously been receiving rehabilitation for several months and encouraged to complete such tasks for herself. Sarah learned only when the step-by-step approach was employed to teach her other self-help skills (see Wilson, 1988, 1999).

Chaining is a procedure whereby tasks or sequences of behaviours are broken down into steps and the steps taught one at a time. Both forward and backward chaining have been used to teach new skills to people with learning disability (Tsoi & Yule, 1980). Forward chaining has been used in cognitive rehabilitation to teach a woman with dysphasia some new words (Moffat, 1989) and backward chaining has been used to teach new routes to a man with the pure amnesic syndrome (Wilson, 1999).

Vanishing cues is a method similar to chaining, in that acquisition of a skill (typically computer terminology) is taught by breaking down the computer terms into individual letters and gradually reducing the number of letters provided (Glisky & Schacter, 1987; Glisky, Schacter & Tulving, 1986; Schacter & Glisky, 1986). In the last-mentioned paper, four patients with amnesia were taught 15 computer-related terms and their definitions through a procedure in which each letter of the word to be learned was one link in the chain. Subjects were provided with fragments of the word (letters) and these were gradually reduced across trials. In this manner, the teaching of the definition of LOOP would be presented as "A repeated segment is called a LOOP". The letters in LOOP would gradually be reduced in the following manner. "A repeated segment is called a LOO–, LO– –, L– – –, – – – –". The subject would be required to complete the segment. Each trial provided one letter less than appeared in the previous trial. All four subjects in this study required fewer letters to complete the words both within and between trials. Furthermore, this method was superior to a repetition control method.

One subject, CH (Glisky & Schacter, 1987), was taught further computer skills sufficient to obtain part-time work as a computer operator. Once the terminology had been learned through the method of vanishing cues, CH practised this in order to speed up her responses to questions about the terminology. A task analysis was then completed to determine what CH would need to learn in order to work at the job that was being offered to her. The task analysis identified the following steps:

1. Document discrimination
2. Acquisition of rules and procedures
3. Simulated job performance in the laboratory
4. Performance in the workplace
5. Task training on: 11 different documents; 14 different programs

Over 250 individual items and components were taught using the method of vanishing cues. This took 6 months to complete but CH was able to carry out her work successfully even though she was unable to recount what her work entailed other than, "It's to do with computers". Glisky (1995) used the same procedure to teach word processing skills to an amnesic patient, and Clare and colleagues have incorporated the method of vanishing cues into teaching names to people with Alzheimer's disease (Clare, Wilson, Breen, & Hodges, 1999; Clare et al., 2000; Clare, Wilson, Carter, Hodges, & Adams, 2001).

Shaping is a procedure based on the idea that a goal can be achieved by reinforcing successive approximations to the target behaviour. It has a long tradition in teaching people with developmental learning disabilities. Tsoi and

Yule (1980) say, "Shaping is an art. It is the art of the therapist, using all the skills and ingenuity at his or her disposal, in getting the handicapped person to produce a novel response. Fortunately, it is an art form which has some ground rules" (p. 68).

The main ground rules are to undertake a careful analysis of the problem; make sure the behaviour is not beyond the capabilities of the person being taught; employ positive reinforcement and other procedures such as prompting, if necessary; and monitor what is happening.

Although not described as "shaping", some successful treatment programmes in cognitive rehabilitation include shaping principles. Alderman and Ward (1991), for example, in their programme to reduce repetitive speech in a brain-injured woman, employed a response cost procedure (described in more detail later in the section on decreasing behaviours). Initially the woman had to retain 36 of the 50 pennies given to her at the start of the session in order to obtain reinforcement; this was later increased to 46 pence.

Paula (described in Wilson, 1999, Ch. 16) was helped to tolerate physiotherapy exercises through a shaping procedure—she was reinforced for spending progressively longer periods on what were for her three difficult exercises.

A further example in which shaping was used to improve the reading and writing skills of a young woman who sustained a severe head injury is provided by Wilson (1989). Maria, 21 years old, was riding pillion on a motorcycle that hit a pedestrian. Maria was thrown backwards, fractured her skull, and sustained damage to her occipital lobes and bruising of the left frontal area. She was admitted to a rehabilitation centre 4 months later. At that time her right eye was closed due to a third nerve palsy, and acuity in the left eye was restricted. It was difficult to assess Maria's visual impairment: although she complained frequently, she never collided with objects, she identified line drawings with relative ease, and counted dots on a card with no hesitation. However, she had difficulty identifying the contents of photographs, and was poor at deciding whether pairs of photographs of people taken from different angles were the same person or not. It is quite possible that Maria had perceptual problems as well as sensory impairment, although the undoubted presence of the latter made it impossible to establish the former conclusively. Maria showed no sign of a reading disorder but, at a distance of 15 inches, she was able to read only when the letters were at least 3 inches high. Her handwriting was very large, with the letters ranging from 2 to $2\frac{1}{2}$ inches high.

The training procedure for Maria was as follows. First, three baselines were taken to establish the maximum distance at which Maria could read four- and five-letter words written in $\frac{3}{4}$-inch-high letters. This distance turned out to be 3 inches. Second, Maria received six training sessions. Non-words were used as training stimuli to reduce both the possibility of guessing and the likelihood of learning the stimuli over repeated presentations. The stimuli were presented on a magnetic board supported in an almost vertical position. Maria sat facing the board with her chin on a chin rest. The stimuli were presented at eye level and the distance from Maria was recorded. She was asked to read each stimulus and given feedback on her performance. After 10 consecutive correct trials the distance from Maria was increased by 2 inches.

By the end of the sixth training session Maria was able to read the non-words at a distance of 15 inches. She was then asked to read 50 new real words. She was able to read these words at a distance of 12–15 inches, which indicated that generalisation had occurred. The handwriting programme was similar. Initially, Maria was asked to keep her letters within parallel lines 2 inches apart. The lines were gradually brought closer together until she was able to write with ¹/₂-inch-high letters.

In some ways this programme seems similar to the de-inhibition or de-blocking programmes described by Luria et al. (1969), and such intervention could provide the explanation for Maria's success. In other words, the poor vision was due to some kind of neural shock which we were able to help her overcome. It is also possible that Maria's problems were wholly or partly hysterical or functional in some way. Although there seems to be no way of resolving these questions, it nevertheless seems likely that shaping procedures are potentially valuable in the treatment of some problems following brain injury.

Another strategy for teaching or improving cognitive skills is expanding rehearsal, also known as spaced retrieval. The information to be recalled (for example, a new telephone number) is presented to the person who is then tested for recall immediately. Success is virtually guaranteed provided that immediate memory span is normal. The person is then tested after a very brief delay (perhaps 2 seconds), then after a slightly longer delay and so on. The gradual extension of the retention interval typically leads to better learning. This fits in with findings that distributed practice leads to better learning than massed practice (Baddeley, 1999; Baddeley & Longman, 1978).

Landauer and Bjork (1978) demonstrated the superiority of expanding rehearsal/spaced retrieval over rote rehearsal or repetition for people without brain injury. Schacter, Rich, and Stampp (1985) demonstrated its effectiveness for people with amnesia. Moffat (1989) used the procedure to reteach words to a patient with Alzheimer's disease and nominal dysphasia. Wilson (1991b) and Camp (2001) both suggest that expanding rehearsal is akin to shaping.

Camp and his colleagues have carried out a number of studies using expanding rehearsal for reducing the problems of people with Alzheimer's disease (AD) (Camp, 1989; Camp, Bird, & Cherry, 2000; Camp, Foss, O'Hanlon, & Stevens, 1996). Clare and colleagues have also incorporated the procedure as one of four methods (along with errorless learning, visual imagery, and vanishing cues) to teach names of friends to VJ, a man diagnosed with AD six years earlier (Clare et al., 1999, 2001).

VJ was 74 years old when first seen. He wanted to relearn the names of people at the social club he attended each week. Photographs of club members

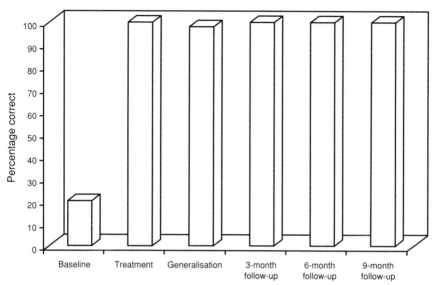

FIG. 5.1   Recall of names by VJ, a man with Alzheimer's disease.

were used to teach the names. Three further photographs were also included—these featured people whose names VJ had not forgotten. These items were considered useful for VJ's motivation and self-esteem. One name was taught each week incorporating expanding rehearsal. Once VJ had worked out a mnemonic for remembering the name, he was then given a vanishing-cues procedure to help learn the name. For example, with the name "Gloria", he was asked to complete the name when the last letter was omitted (e.g., GLORI–), then when the last two letters were omitted (GLOR– –) and so forth. Once the whole name was completed, VJ was asked to recall the name following increasingly long intervals (e.g., 30 s, 1 min, 2 min, etc.). He was asked not to guess if he did not know the name (which was written on the back of the photograph in case he needed to check).

The mean recall score during the baseline period was 20%. This increased to 98% following intervention and generalisation (VJ was shown the photographs and was asked to identify each person from the relevant photograph and to introduce each by name to the psychologist). At 3-month, 6-month, and 9-month follow-up VJ's recall of the 11 names was 100%. He practised the names daily with the photographs and saw the people at his club weekly during this time (see Figure 5.1).

After 9 months, VJ was asked to stop practising. He returned the photographs and was tested weekly during the following year and monthly for a further year. Following the death of one of the club members, one photograph was removed leaving 10 "trained" names. Over the next year, VJ's recall of these 10 names ranged from 10 to 5 with a mean of 8. During the second year he ranged from 9 to 5 with a trend towards fewer names recalled over time. Even without daily practice, however, VJ did not return to baseline levels despite the fact that his disease was progressing.

Positive reinforcement is one of the major behavioural procedures for improving behaviours. It has been called one of the most powerful methods in behaviour modification (Hemsley & Carr, 1980) and certainly has an important place in the management of problems following brain injury. Lincoln (1978) said that praise, rest, and attention are powerful reinforcers in rehabilitation. Secondary reinforcers such as tokens (Alderman & Ward, 1991; Wood, 1984), trips to the hydrotherapy pool (Wilson, 1981), pub lunches (Wilson, 1991c), favourite picture books about horses, and access to motorcycle magazines have also been used (Wilson, 1999).

The importance of selecting the right reinforcer for people with little motivation and/or reduced states of awareness was brought home during the development of the Wessex Head Injury Matrix (WHIM) (Shiel et al., 2000a, 2000b; see also Chapter 4). One of the 88 people observed during the development of the WHIM was Bennie, a 34-year-old man who had sustained a severe head injury some 9 months earlier. Bennie was very unresponsive, his eyes were open, he had a sleep–wake cycle and he was considered to be minimally conscious. Thus he failed to respond to events in the environment. He spent his day in bed with his head turned to the left. His mother told the research team that before his accident Bennie was passionately interested in cars and car racing. A video of car racing and several car racing magazines were purchased and an experiment was set up. A video player was placed to the right of Bennie's bed and the car racing video inserted. Bennie, who had never been known to turn his head to the right since his accident, turned to look at the video. When the video was switched off, his head returned to the left. The video was switched on once more and, again, he turned his head to the right. The procedure was repeated many times during that session and others. Sometimes the magazines were used and again the same response occurred. If Bennie's head turned within 30 seconds on three consecutive occasions during the same session, we considered this to be a reliable response. Bennie responded reliably to the videos and magazines for several weeks until his sudden and unexpected death soon afterwards.

Bennie and others in the same study showed us that some people who have recently emerged from coma after a severe head injury require reinforcers particularly important to them in order to encourage them to respond or engage with others in their environment. One man showed no evidence of comprehension, until he was offered a £10 note (Watson & Horn, 1991). He reached out and took the note, much to the surprise of Martin Watson who was testing him. Martin did not expect the man to do this. "Oh," said Martin, "that was just a test, it's my money and I need it back!" The man laughed and returned the money. Obviously, this man was comprehending some things but apparently had not been motivated or stimulated enough to respond to other events or people.

The final procedure we want to touch on here is goal planning, already described in Chapter 3. Goal planning is not new and has been used in behavioural modification for many years. What is relatively recent is the growth and acceptance of goal planning as the basic approach in many rehabilitation centres in the United Kingdom and other places. Most British rehabilitation centres incorporate goal planning as a strategy for all clients. Goals to be attained by discharge are negotiated between patients, families, and staff on admission. As described earlier, in Chapter 3, short-term goals (action plans) are set each week or fortnight as a means to achieve the long-term goals.

One recent example of successful goal planning, to help Mark, a man with memory problems, is described by Wilson, Evans, and Williams (in press). Mark was 30 years old when he sustained a severe head injury. He was on a mountain bike holiday in Switzerland and fell 1000 feet down a mountain. He was airlifted to a specialist hospital. A CT scan showed diffuse axonal injury, oedema, small deep midline haemorrhages, and a subdural haematoma. The haematoma was evacuated via a burrhole. Mark was in coma for 1 week and in post traumatic amnesia for a further week. He contracted meningitis, pneumonia, and septicaemia. He had a tracheostomy tube inserted for 10 days. Some 3 weeks post-injury Mark was transferred to an acute rehabilitation centre in London. He was ataxic and agitated and needed two people to help him stand from a sitting position. He made a good physical recovery in London but 9 months later remained with significant cognitive problems. At this point he was admitted to the Oliver Zangwill Centre for Neuropsychological Rehabilitation.

The referral form noted that Mark needed help with memory, attention, and planning problems. He was described as lacking initiative compared to his premorbid personality. He had some insight into his difficulties but did not appreciate the nature and extent of his memory problems and the potential impact of such impairments on his work. On assessment, Mark's intellectual ability was in the average to above-average range (we estimated above-average functioning premorbidly). He had particular problems with memory, together with some mild executive deficits.

With the rehabilitation team, Mark set some specific goals for his programme, which lasted 20 weeks, the first 10 weeks being intensive (i.e., 5 days per week) and the second 10 weeks being divided between home, work, and the rehabilitation centre. The goals for his programme were (1) to develop an awareness of his strengths and weaknesses in a written form consistent with his neuropsychological profile and describe how any problems would impact on domestic, social, and work situations; (2) to identify whether he could return to his previous employment; (3) to manage his financial affairs independently; (4) to demonstrate competence in negotiation skills as rated by a work colleague; (5) to develop a range of leisure interests. To achieve these goals Mark engaged in a programme consisting of both group work (e.g., Understanding Brain Injury Group, Memory Group, Planning/Problem Solving Group) and work with individual team members.

There were many elements to Mark's programme, but one of the most critical was helping him cope with memory difficulties. His insight into these problems was achieved by education about the nature of memory and the problems that may exist after brain injury (through an Understanding Brain Injury Group and a Memory Group). He was given feedback from the result of standardised assessments. He was asked (prompted and monitored) to keep a diary of memory errors. He was asked to consider his work role and to identify the demands on memory that were made as part of his work. He developed better insight into his difficulties, which had a "down-side" in that he began to feel low, as he became less confident that he would be able to return to work. However, the rehabilitation team supported him in developing a set of strategies designed to compensate for the problems. He adopted these strategies successfully. He used, and continues to use, a large diary for appointments and "things to do". He began to use a computer "contacts" card system for recording relevant information about brokers who came to him with business. He also learned to use mnemonic strategies for remembering people's names and other information. Mark recognised that the ability to judge risk effectively was the essence of his premorbid success as an underwriter, and that his ability to do this depended on picking up on and remembering pieces of information about locations (e.g., earthquake zones), companies, and other bodies that might present a risk. To compensate for his memory in relation to this issue, he developed and continually updated a database of information about insurance risks (i.e., details of major losses/disasters compiled from the Lloyds list of such losses), to which he could refer when assessing risk associated with new business. Many of these strategies might be used by the non-memory-impaired underwriter, but Mark had previously been successful without any of them. For this reason he had to go through the process of appreciating the nature of his difficulties, accepting the need for memory aids, implementing strategies, and evaluating their value.

Critical to Mark's successful return to work was, we believe, a programme of step-wise increases in the level of work responsibilities. Initially he shadowed other underwriters, who would ask him for his views on business offered to them by brokers. Next he undertook "minimal risk" business such as insurance renewals. Following this he was able to make underwriting decisions, but these had to be checked by his manager. Finally he was given full underwriting authority. This staged approach was necessary for a variety of reasons. It allowed his manager to develop confidence in Mark's judgement in a high-risk business. It enabled Mark to develop his confidence. It also allowed time for him to learn to apply the strategies he had developed to compensate for memory problems.

Seven months after beginning his rehabilitation programme, Mark was reinstated on the company payroll and after a further 12 months he remains employed. He continues to use the strategies he learned, which he reports are absolutely necessary to his success at work. By being in work he contributes to the cost of his rehabilitation through the tax he pays on his salary and through the tax his company pays as a result of Mark's success in his work. By being in work, welfare costs are also saved. Not all patients undertaking rehabilitation are in a position to make such clinical or financial gains. While it might seem unethical to judge the value of rehabilitation by its cost-effectiveness, cases such as Mark's illustrate that rehabilitation can be both clinically and cost-effective.

Finally in this section it must be pointed out that these strategies are not mutually exclusive. A combination of positive reinforcement and other strategies such as prompting, chaining, or shaping can be used. These approaches are similar to each other because each of them gradually works towards achievement of a final goal.

BEHAVIOURAL APPROACHES FOR DECREASING OR ELIMINATING INAPPROPRIATE BEHAVIOURS

Some inappropriate behaviours such as distractibility, anxiety, fear, and poor self-esteem are common after brain injury. Less common are severe disruptive behaviours, which are not covered in this book and readers interested in this topic should see Alderman (2001), Alderman, Davies, Jones, and McDonnel (1999), Wood (1987, 1988, 1990). Less severe problems are dealt with in the following chapter.

Emotional problems may be due to organic or non-organic causes. People sustaining brain stem strokes, for example, may show marked fluctuations in their behaviour perhaps ranging from tears to laughter several times over in the space of a few minutes. Emotional problems may also result from non-organic causes such as fear of what might happen, grief at the loss of one's previous intellectual level of functioning, panic because of loss of memory, and reduced self-esteem because of changes in physical appearance, motor ability, or reduced intellectual powers.

It is not always easy to distinguish between emotional and cognitive problems, and an interaction between the two may frequently occur. One stroke patient, for example, was referred to the psychology department by her physiotherapist because she was extremely frightened both of walking and of transferring from her wheelchair to elsewhere. Following neuropsychological assessments and observations in physiotherapy, it transpired that the woman's fear stemmed from her inability to judge depth and distance. She thought that people 10 feet away were going to bump into her, and when lying on a mat on the floor in the physiotherapy department, she thought she would fall down several feet and hurt herself. Obviously treatment in such cases will need to take into account both emotional and cognitive factors.

Fear, anxiety, depression, and social isolation are faced by many brain-injured people. Prigatano (1995, 2000) believes that dealing with the emotional effects of brain injury is essential to rehabilitation success. Holistic programmes always include treatment for both emotional and cognitive problems (Wilson, 1997a). Depression and anxiety may be expected in about two-thirds of people with traumatic brain injury (TBI) (McKinlay, Brooks, Bond, Martinage, & Marshall, 1981). Kopelman and Crawford (1996) found 40% of 200 consecutive referrals to a memory clinic showed signs of clinical depression, and Evans and Wilson (1992) found anxiety common in people referred to a memory group. People with brain injury are also likely to suffer social isolation (Talbott, 1989; Wilson, 1991a). Emotional changes are also seen in stroke patients. Those with right hemisphere lesions are likely to show denial or indifference to their problems (Weinstein, 1991), whereas those with left hemisphere lesions are more likely to show a "catastrophic reaction". These are in addition to the problems resulting from non-organic causes mentioned earlier. Post traumatic stress disorder is increasingly recognised after TBI (McMillan, Jongen, & Greenwood, 1996) and may be an important part of cognitive rehabilitation. Because emotion affects how we think and behave, rehabilitation should address all these aspects.

In an excellent review of emotional and psychosocial problems after brain injury, Gainotti (1993) distinguishes three main factors causing these problems. First, there is neurological damage, which may provoke disturbances through the disruption of the specific neural mechanisms subserving the regulation and control of emotional and social behaviour. Second, there are psychological or psychodynamic factors involving attitudes towards disability and implications for quality of life. Third, there are the consequences of functional impairment on the patient's social network and social activities. Most clinical psychologists and some neuropsychologists are well able to deal with the emotional and social consequences of brain injury through anxiety-management procedures, cognitive therapy, family therapy, and social skills training.

Although behavioural approaches to the management of mood and emotional disorders following brain injury will be covered, to a large extent, in Chapter 6, some of these disorders that impact on cognitive functioning, particularly those involving reduction of fear, anxiety, and other inappropriate behaviours, will be discussed here.

Reducing anxiety is a big part of many rehabilitation programmes. Evans and Wilson (1992) suggest that one of the main advantages of attendance at a memory group is anxiety reduction. Wilson (1999) describes one young man, Jack, whose scores on the Hospital Anxiety and Depression Scale (HAD; Zigmond & Snaith, 1983) were originally very high on the anxiety section but rapidly declined once he started attending memory group sessions.

The stroke patient described earlier, whose fear of walking and transferring resulted from loss of depth perception, was helped to reduce her anxiety and fear through the provision of tactile support. A rope was placed around the walls of her rooms for her to hold on to when moving about. If she had to cross a room or cross the garden she was provided with a shopping cart to hold on to. This considerably reduced her anxiety. Further discussion of mood disorders can be found in Chapter 7.

Another behavioural strategy mentioned earlier is "response cost", whereby tokens are deducted for undesirable behaviours. This is in contrast to the usual procedure of awarding tokens (points, stars, discs, etc.) for appropriate behaviour (Murphy & Oliver, 1987). Alderman and Ward (1991) used a response cost procedure with a 36-year-old woman who had survived herpes simplex encephalitis a year earlier. She presented with a dysexecutive syndrome and severe behaviour disorders including repetitive speech (for example, "You will give me some chocolate won't you, won't you, you will be sure to give me some chocolate won't you, won't you . . ."). In one 5-hour period 985 episodes of repetitive speech were recorded.

Treatment sessions were carried out for 1 hour a day, 5 days a week using a reversal (A-B-A-C-A-CD) design. A represented the baseline period: B was treatment 1 (response cost—the woman was issued with 50 one-pence pieces; she had to give 1 to the therapist each time she engaged in repetitive speech and needed at least 36 to obtain a reward at the end of the session); C represented treatment 2 (modified response cost as before, except that the woman was now required to retain 46 pence in order to obtain her reward); CD represented treatment 3 (modified response cost as before plus cognitive overlearning whereby the woman was prompted to repeat the statement "I must not repeat myself" continuously for 1 minute). The results can be seen in Figure 5.2 and show that the woman's repetitive speech decreased significantly following treatment. This improvement was maintained for at least 3 months post treatment.

It may sound strange that one of the treatment components required the woman to repeat herself for 1 minute when the aim of treatment was to reduce repetitive speech. It would appear that she found this procedure aversive when the therapist required the woman to repeat herself, whereas when the woman herself initiated repetition she found this pleasurable or motivating.

Alderman et al. (1995) report a different treatment for another woman with repetitive speech, also following herpes simplex encephalitis. Response cost was used on the ward but found not to generalise to other environments. To reduce her speech when away from the ward a method called "self-monitoring training" was used. This consisted of five stages (each of which took place during a 20-minute walk in the hospital grounds). A therapist recorded all utterances independently. Stage 1 was the baseline during which an average of 4.1 utterances per minute was recorded. The second stage was spontaneous self-monitoring to see how successfully the woman (SK) could self-monitor her own utterances. She was given a digital counter to record these. Replies to questions from the accompanying therapist were not required to be monitored. Stage 3 involved prompted self-monitoring. The procedure was similar to Stage 2 except that if

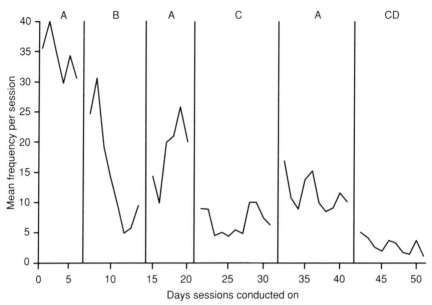

FIG. 5.2   Treatment of repetitive speech using response cost and cognitive overlearning. A, no treatment; B, response cost; C, modified response cost; CD, modified response cost and cognitive overlearning. [From Alderman, N., & Ward, A. (1991). Behavioural treatment of the dysexecutive syndrome: Reduction of repetitive speech using response cost and cognitive overlearning. *Neuropsychological Rehabilitation*, *1*, p. 72. Reproduced by permission of Psychology Press and Dr N. Alderman.]

SK did not spontaneously record an utterance the therapist prompted her. Stage 4 involved independent self-monitoring and reinforcement (a trip to the hospital café) provided that SK's record was within 50% of the therapist's independent record. The final stage required SK to monitor independently and to meet an agreed target that was gradually reduced. The results can be seen in Figure 5.3.

Alderman and Ward (1991) and Alderman et al. (1995) suggest that these behavioural methods work with patients with dysexecutive syndrome because such patients have increased distractibility, difficulties monitoring their own performance, and problems in utilising feedback. Thus they may be unaware of the inappropriateness of their own behaviour and may not be able to recognise or respond to the social cues of others to change their behaviour. Both response cost and self-monitoring training appear to facilitate learning by directing the patients' attention to aspects of their behaviour they are not monitoring. In addition, salient feedback is presented in an exaggerated form to the patient and thus increases awareness. A later paper by Alderman (1996) also demonstrates that exaggerated feedback can improve the performance of dysexecutive patients on tasks requiring divided attention.

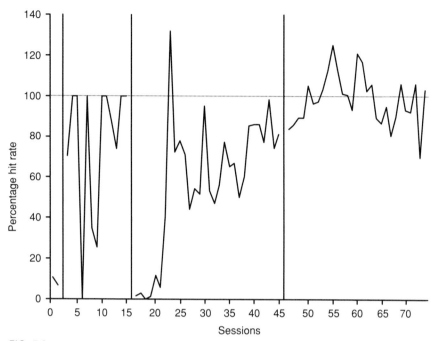

FIG. 5.3   Percentage agreement in recordings made during SMT sessions by SK and her therapist of the frequency of self-initiated verbal utterances. The dotted line represents perfect agreement (100%). Values greater than 100% represent either an over-zealous response or perseveration. [From Alderman, N., Fry, R. K., & Youngson, H. A. (1995). Improvement of self-monitoring skills, reduction of behaviour disturbance and the dysexecutive syndrome: Comparison of response cost and a new programme of self-monitoring training. *Neuropsychological Rehabilitation*, *5*, p. 210. Reproduced by permission of Psychology Press and Dr N. Alderman.]

One method worth considering for people with cognitive deficits and inappropriate behaviours is that of "stimulus control". In other words, because problem behaviours may only occur in certain situations, changing the situation may eliminate the problem behaviour. Although this method is probably most likely to be used for people with developmental learning difficulties (Murphy & Oliver, 1987), it has a place in cognitive rehabilitation. People who are extremely distractible because of severe attention deficits may do better if placed in situations with no or minimal distractions such as a room with no other patients, no unnecessary materials, no windows to glance out of, and so forth. Obviously this scenario is no good as a long-term solution, but as a starting point to help focus attention it may be ideal.

It is more common in cognitive rehabilitation to modify or restructure the environment in some way in order to avoid or bypass cognitive difficulties. People with severe impairments of planning and organisational skills may benefit from working in a structured environment where no demands are made on them, where it is clear what is required of them, and where they do not have to "think on their feet".

Although ideally one would want to teach severely impaired people how to cope with new situations and new problems, in some circumstances the best solution might be environmental modification. For example, people who are in danger of burning themselves, or setting fire to the house because they forget to switch off appliances, can be provided with irons, cookers, kettles, electric lights, and so forth that turn themselves off after a certain interval to reduce such dangers. People who may forget how many tablets they have taken may require someone to give them their tablets at a certain time, or be provided with an automatic dispenser. If someone is always losing the house key, it is possible to clip the key to a belt. Jim (Wilson, 1999, Ch. 20) was very disruptive in his occupational therapy sessions until his environment was changed by giving him simpler tasks to do. Richard, (Wilson, 1999, Ch. 18),who had severe visuospatial difficulties, was unable to find his mug or his socks until the mug was placed alone on a higher shelf and his socks placed in a separate drawer from his other clothes.

People just emerging from coma and in states of agitation may be helped by reducing stimulation in the environment. In some wards there may be considerable noise from radios, televisions, and people talking, the lights may be very bright, and there may be large numbers of people around. In these circumstances moving the person to a quiet room, with little noise, reduced lighting, and just one or two assistants may reduce or eliminate the agitation and calm the person down.

One patient, for whom the only real help we could give was by restructuring the environment, is also described in Wilson (1999, Ch. 6). This was Clive, a man with an extremely severe memory impairment. A student working with Clive in 1991, intrigued by Clive's regular bouts of belching and jerking, carried out a systematic observation and noticed that a belch or jerk was more likely to occur following a change in activity such as moving position from sitting to walking, or moving from one task, such as playing the piano, to another, such as playing cards. When assessing Clive, it was also noticed that changing from one test or one subtest to another would also provoke an outburst of belching or jerking. Although not possible to prevent all changes in activity, it was possible to help Clive remain calmer by ensuring that the changes were as few as possible. Other strategies found to help Clive involved stimulus control/environmental modification. Thus people addressed him by his surname (Mr W____) rather than his first name. This was because we were all strangers to Clive, he never remembered meeting people before, and became irritated if strangers were too familiar and addressed him as "Clive". It was also inadvisable to sympathise with his very frequent statements that he had "just woken up". If one replied "That must be distressing" or "So you feel you have just woken up?", he became increasingly agitated. Changing the topic of conversation, on the other hand, typically avoided such agitation. Similarly, if one tried to persuade him that he had not just woken up (e.g., "Look at this videotape of you—you were obviously awake then"), Clive became angry, so it was easier and kinder to avoid such confrontation.

In short, people interacting with Clive learned to modify their own behaviour and found better ways to manage and relate to him. This was a variation of the environmental modification approach in that those around Clive adjusted the verbal and social environments for him, enabling him to manage without too much agitation and anger.

A programme involving cognitive rehabilitation for memory deficits and cognitive behaviour therapy for an obsessive compulsive disorder was reported by Williams, Evans, and Wilson (2000). The programme was designed for a young man, Carl, who was involved in a road traffic accident at the age of 21 years. He was in a coma for 4 weeks and in post traumatic amnesia for 2–3 months. Three years later Carl was admitted to the Oliver Zangwill Centre for help with his memory problems and his emotional problems. Because of his poor memory, Carl said he did not "trust himself" to remember activities, he checked things frequently (e.g., whether the door was locked, whether he had his keys). He was also socially isolated and frightened that if he became more active he would hurt himself. He was both anxious and depressed.

Carl attended the rehabilitation programme for 4 months. Each day he attended both group and individual sessions. One group (Understanding Brain Injury) was designed to improve Carl's insight into his strengths and weaknesses. He attended a memory group as well as having individual memory rehabilitation sessions. In the sessions he was taught strategies, in particular the use of a filofax for planning ahead, the use of a voice organiser to help him remember what had happened (he used the voice organiser to record telephone conversations), and the use of an electronic organiser to remind him to do things such as take exercise and make a telephone call. He was taught to try to "burn-in" a mental image of locking the door, putting away his key, and so on, in order to reduce his need to check.

Carl also attended sessions on stress management. These included breathing exercises and identifying hierarchies that he could work through to help him socialise and go out to places in the community. Each week goals were set (e.g., visit the pub/social centre/swimming pool). He was given vocational counselling and introduced to a local college where he started a computer course. By the time of discharge, Carl was attending college, socialising (including going to the pub and clubs) two to three times a week, independent in the local and wider community, checking far less often, and expressing greater trust in himself to remember things.

Evans et al. (1998) describe another patient who showed signs of an obsessive compulsive disorder. She spent an excessively long time in the bath each day (typically 1 hour and 20 minutes), where she engaged in a ritual of having to wash each of 31 body zones for a particular length of time. Despite agreeing to spend no longer than 30 minutes in the bath, she consistently failed to reduce the time, often because she lost track of which zone she was washing and how many times she had washed that zone. She was asked to cut down the 31 zones to 9 (e.g., her two arms became one zone instead of two), to use a checklist to record when each zone was completed, and to record the amount of time spent on each zone. This led to a reduction in the time in the bath from 80 minutes to 40. Another aid, NeuroPage® (Wilson, Emslie, Quirk, & Evans, 2001b; Wilson, Evans, Emslie, & Malinek, 1997), helped to reduce her distractibility. For example, she would set off to water the plants but stop to count the cars going past the window, or intend to start cooking a meal but start doing something else on the way. When the bleep on the pager sounded, however, and the message appeared "water the plants" or "plan the meal", she invariably carried out the task without becoming side-tracked.

Finally, we address errorless learning in cognitive rehabilitation—or at least in one aspect of cognitive rehabilitation—the rehabilitation of memory disorders. We do not yet know whether errorless learning is better than trial-and-error learning for cognitive disorders other than memory. Errorless learning is a teaching technique whereby people are prevented, as far as possible, from making mistakes while they are learning a new skill or acquiring new information. Instead of teaching by demonstration, which may involve the learner in trial-and-error, the experimenter, therapist, or teacher presents the correct information or procedure in ways that minimise the possibility of erroneous responses.

There are two theoretical backgrounds to investigations of errorless learning in people with organic memory impairment. The first is the work on errorless discrimination learning from the field of behavioural psychology, first described by Terrace in the 1960s (Terrace, 1963, 1966). Terrace was working with pigeons and found that it was possible to teach pigeons to discriminate a red key from a green key with a teaching technique whereby the pigeons made no (or very few) errors during learning. Furthermore, the pigeons learning via errorless learning were reported to show less emotional behaviour than the pigeons who learned with trial-and-error learning.

Sidman and Stoddard (1967) applied errorless learning principles to children with developmental learning difficulties. They were able to teach these children to discriminate ellipses from circles. Others soon took up the idea (e.g., Cullen, 1976; Jones & Eayrs, 1992; Walsh & Lamberts, 1979). Cullen (1976) believed that if errors were made during learning it was harder to remember just what had been learned. He also pointed out that more reinforcement occurred during errorless learning as only successes occurred, never failures. To this day errorless learning is a frequently used teaching technique for people with developmental learning difficulties.

The second theoretical impetus came from studies of implicit memory and implicit learning from cognitive psychology and cognitive neuropsychology (e.g., Brooks & Baddeley, 1976; Graf & Schacter, 1985; Tulving & Schacter, 1990, and many others). Although it has been known for decades that memory-impaired people can learn some skills and information normally through their intact (or relatively intact) implicit learning abilities, it has been difficult to apply this knowledge to reduce the real-life problems encountered by people with organic memory deficits.

Glisky and colleagues (Glisky & Schacter, 1987; Glisky et al., 1986) tried to capitalise on intact implicit abilities to teach people with amnesia computer terminology using a technique they called "the method of vanishing cues". Despite some successes, the method of vanishing cues involved considerable time and effort both from the experimenters and the people with amnesia. Implicit memory or learning, on the other hand, does not involve effort as it occurs without conscious recollection. This, together with certain other anomalies seen during implicit learning (such as the observation that in a fragmented picture/perceptual priming procedure, if an amnesic patient mislabels a fragment during an early presentation, the error may "stick" and be repeated on successive presentations) led Baddeley and Wilson (1994) to ask the question "Do amnesic patients learn better if prevented from making mistakes during the learning process?". In a study with 16 young and 16 elderly control participants, and 16 densely amnesic people, employing a stem-completion procedure, it was found that every one of the amnesic people learned better if prevented from making mistakes during learning.

Baddeley and Wilson (1994) believed errorless learning was superior to trial-and-error because it depended on implicit memory. As amnesic people could not use explicit memory effectively, they were forced to rely on implicit memory. This system is not designed to eliminate errors, so it is better to prevent the injection of errors in the first place. In the absence of an efficient episodic memory, the very fact of making an incorrect response may strengthen or reinforce the error.

Errorless learning principles were quickly adopted in the rehabilitation of memory-impaired people. Wilson, Baddeley, Evans, and Shiel (1994) described a number of single-case studies in which amnesic people were taught several tasks such as learning therapists' names, learning to programme an electronic organiser, and learning to recognise objects. Each participant was taught two similar tasks in an errorful or an errorless way. In each case errorless was superior to errorful learning. Wilson and Evans (1996) provided further support for these findings. Squires, Hunkin, and Parkin (1996) taught a man with amnesia to use a notebook with an errorless learning procedure. The same group (Squires, Aldrich, Parkin, & Hunkin, 1998; Squires et al., 1997) found that errorless learning procedures enabled amnesic people to learn novel associations, and to acquire word processing skills. More recently, these principles have been used successfully with people with Alzheimer's disease (Clare et al., 1999, 2000, 2001). One of these patients, VJ, was described earlier in the chapter.

Although Baddeley and Wilson (1994) believe the efficacy of errorless learning is due to the fact that it depends on implicit memory, there are alternative explanations. Hunkin, Squires, Parkin, and Tidy (1998) believe it is due to the effects of error prevention on the residual explicit memory capacities of people with amnesia. A third explanation is that it is due to both implicit and explicit systems. Ongoing work in Cambridge (Page, Wilson, Norris, Shiel, & Carter, 2001; Wilson, Carter, Norris, & Page, 2001a) suggests that this third explanation is probably true. For people with very severe impairment (and thus no or very little explicit memory), implicit memory is almost certainly responsible. For those with less severe impairment and some episodic memory functioning, errorless learning can also strengthen residual explicit memory.

CONCLUSIONS

When using behavioural approaches with people who have sustained an injury or insult to the brain, we need to take into account neurological, neuropsychological, emotional, and phenomenological factors.

It is important to acknowledge and be informed about the contributions that other branches of psychology, medicine, linguistics, and so forth can offer. Within psychology, neuropsychology enables us to understand the organisation of the brain and cognitive psychology has provided models of cognitive functioning to conceptualise, explain, and predict certain phenomena. Behavioural psychology has contributed most by generating new techniques for treatment. It has provided us with a technology of learning based on careful observation and a concern for behavioural change.

The combination of measurement and treatment together with single-case experimental designs has provided psychologists and therapists with some powerful strategies that lend themselves well to the treatment of people with cognitive problems resulting from damage to the brain.

CHAPTER 6

Behavioural approaches to disruptive disorders

Most people who sustain a brain injury subsequently exhibit some forms of emotional and behavioural change in addition to their cognitive problems. These changes vary in severity and where they are more subtle, relatives and carers often find it difficult to describe exactly what has changed. This chapter will consider the management of irritability and aggression, and that of disinhibited or inappropriate behaviour, including sexual disinhibition. These are both areas that disrupt treatment programmes and contribute significantly to the stress experienced by families and to the success or otherwise of reintegration into the community.

BEHAVIOURAL MANAGEMENT OF AGGRESSION

Irritability and aggression are among the most common sequelae noted by relatives following brain injury. Severe verbal or physical aggression can occur during the period of acute medical care as the individual regains consciousness but remains in an agitated and confused state. This can be particularly frightening for family members as it is often out of character and seemingly out of control. Staff too can find it difficult to manage a high level of agitated behaviour on a busy medical ward. Difficult patterns of behaviours can be unintentionally reinforced, which in turn can create problems in later stages of rehabilitation.

During the sub-acute phases of rehabilitation, aggressive behaviours may develop as the patient is unable to complete previously routine tasks and cannot understand or interpret the surrounding environment. Fear and frustration can manifest themselves as aggression. At this stage the behaviour is often accompanied by a belief, usually on the part of the patient but sometimes supported by family members, that discharge from hospital to the home environment will resolve the situation. However, the problems may continue and other aggressive behaviours can develop following discharge. The strains of everyday living may be too much for the patient, again resulting in episodes of frustration developing into verbal and physical aggression.

In its most severe manifestations, aggression can result in admission to specialist units for treatment. Specialist units such as the Kemsley Unit at St Andrews Hospital, Northampton, have established highly structured and consistent programmes using token economies and fixed reinforcement schedules (Wood & Eames, 1981). These programmes have demonstrated considerable success in containing and modifying severe behavioural disturbance. For most families, however, the experience is one of daily strain, of a household "walking on eggshells", which can ultimately become unbearable and result in family breakdown. Behavioural techniques that involve self-control and self-instruction can form the basis of less intensive programmes in outpatient and community settings. Here the approach can be extended to the large number of patients who seek to regain a place in their community or work place and who find that their emotional and behavioural deficits are preventing successful reintegration.

Behavioural approaches for aggressive behaviour

Behavioural interventions for aggressive behaviour seek to modify (1) what happens before the outburst (antecedent controls), (2) what happens after the outburst (consequent controls), and/or (3) the individual's approach to controlling their own behaviour. In practice many treatment programmes will involve elements of all three approaches.

Antecedent controls

Decreasing stimulation. This approach is particularly useful at an early stage post-injury during the period of agitation and confusion. Agitation can be precipitated by noise, the presence of too many people, therapy that is placing too many demands, or simply fatigue. Removing some of these environmental factors may be sufficient to reduce the problem. For example, where a number of staff are required to carry out a specific procedure, it is useful to ensure that only one staff member talks during the interaction to avoid over-stimulation. This is more readily achievable in an organised and structured environment where identified staff are allocated to and familiar with each case. It is harder to implement in other settings such as general medical wards.

Increasing predictability. There are many examples where aggression occurs when the patient has forgotten something or failed to predict an event. By chaining events together and by planning an intervention carefully it is possible to compensate for the memory loss or failure of organisational ability, and to redirect the patient's attention early in the course of escalating aggressive behaviours. This is an approach that can be helpful both in the early stages of rehabilitation where the memory problems may be very apparent, and also later in community programmes where cognitive failures may be only one of several antecedents for the aggressive outburst (Feeney & Ylvisaker 1995).

Signalling an impending event. When an event appears to happen "out of the blue" it can contribute to the sense of confusion and frustration that often underlies the aggressive outbursts. Talking to the patient and explaining the procedure that is about to be performed is one way of reducing aggressive responses. Reducing the element of surprise is also helpful in reducing agitation. For example, a 74-year-old lady in a nursing home who was referred for assessment of aggressive behaviour was found to have a left homonymous hemianopia and neglect. Behavioural observation identified that if nursing staff approached the patient from the neglected side she would usually hit out. If the staff approached the patient from the side not affected by visual neglect no physical aggression occurred.

Consequent controls

Reinforce good behaviour. The simplest and most widely applicable form of positive reinforcement is social reinforcement—giving someone praise, encouragement, or attention—when they are not being aggressive. If applied consistently and appropriately it can be sufficient to shape and sustain desirable behaviours. Material reinforcements in the form of food, money, or privileges can also be used, although they have to be tailored to the needs of the person whose behaviour is being modified. Within a token economy or where points are awarded for non-aggression or positive behaviours within a fixed interval of time, the points or tokens earned may subsequently be exchanged for material rewards (Blackerby, 1988; Wood, 1988).

Differential reinforcement. Here the aggressive behaviour is selectively ignored and other behaviours incompatible with aggression are reinforced. This may require training for the patient in selection and completion of alternative behaviours, as many brain-injured people also demonstrate poor problem solving and limited generation of ideas (Alderman & Knight, 1997; Hegel & Ferguson, 2000).

Response cost. This is based on the principle of negative reinforcement and involves the removal of something of value every time a defined target behaviour occurs, leading to a decrease in the frequency of that behaviour. Immediate withdrawal of tokens or rewards in response to specific behaviours has been found to be particularly useful where there are gross cognitive deficits that interfere with normal contingent learning. Although learning theory would predict that this type of reinforcement would render the behavioural change susceptible to extinction on withdrawal of the reward system, some success has been achieved by employing the use of verbal mediation strategies and negative learning, described previously by Wood (1987) as cognitive overlearning. For a more detailed account of this approach see Alderman and Burgess (1990) and Alderman and Ward (1991).

Time out from positive reinforcement.   Time out involves placing the patient in a situation that will not allow him or her to come into contact with specific stimuli or consequences. It may involve removing the patient to a "time out" room (exclusion) or withdrawing from interaction with the patient for an identified period of time whilst leaving them in the original setting (non-exclusion). Both exclusionary time out (Goodman-Smith & Turnbull, 1983) and non-exclusionary time out have been used (Wood, 1987) in the context of an ongoing programme of positive reinforcement for non-aggressive behaviours.

Presentation of aversive stimuli and physical restraint.   These approaches are less common but there are a number of case examples reported in the literature. Wood (1987) described the use of aromatic ammonia vapour to reduce spitting frequency, an unpleasant throat-clearing habit, and exaggerated nose-picking in a head-injured adult. Negative verbal feedback and physical restraint have been combined (Jacobs, Lynch, Cornick, & Slifer 1986; McMillan, Papadopoulos, Cornall, & Greenwood 1990). McMillan et al. (1990) describe an intervention to address violent and sexually disinhibited behaviour together with poor self-care in a 38-year-old teacher following herpes simplex encephalitis. Both treatment programmes were implemented by a special (psychiatric) nurse. Physical restraint was used following each violent incident and the patient was held for 30 seconds or until she ceased to struggle. A food reward was given if she was not violent for a period of 30 minutes. The incidence of violent behaviour reduced from up to 55 times per day to zero over a 2-month period. Sexual disinhibition was treated only after the violent behaviour no longer occurred. Non-verbal behaviour such as touching was initially treated by raising a finger and shouting "No!" immediately and with no further social or verbal reinforcement for a few minutes. As before she was rewarded with a food item if not exhibiting the behaviour over a period of 1 hour. Sexual disinhibition was eliminated in supervised settings, but continued to occur if the patient was left unsupervised.

Self-management techniques

Anxiety-management techniques.   Patients can be trained in the use of self-monitoring of anxiety levels and to implement a range of relaxation techniques to reduce agitation before it escalates to a more aggressive response. Burgess and Alderman (1990) taught one patient to monitor his anxiety levels, to restructure his cognitions surrounding the anxiety, and "mastery" skills that gave him greater control over his personal care. At a 3-month follow-up the patient's shouting had shown some relapse but had not returned to baseline levels.

Self-control and problem solving.   Learning to identify problems, to generate alternative solutions, and to select appropriate solutions can be effective (Burke, Wesolowski, & Lane, 1988b; Foxx, Marchand-Martella, Martella, Braunling-McMorrow, & McMorrow, 1988; Foxx et al., 1989). Some programmes concentrate specifically on certain skills, for example, anger management (McKinlay & Hickox, 1988; O'Leary, 2000) or stress inoculation (Lira, Carne, & Masri, 1983; Zencius & Wesolowski, 1989) where the patients are taught ways to cope with anger-provoking situations together with training in the application of these techniques in a hierarchy of actual anger-related situations. Zencius and Wesolowski (1989) treated a 28-year-old woman whose response to agitation was to run away from the home or work situation. They taught her to identify when she was becoming agitated, i.e., through muscle tension and emotional outbursts, to remove herself from that environment, and then to self-initiate relaxation strategies. During the training period the frequency of elopements fell from a mean of 2.2 per week to 0.1 per week, and at 6-week follow-up the frequency was 0. Follow-up more than 4 months later did not identify any further incidents.

Behavioural management of aggression in community settings

One of the major pitfalls in behavioural management in any setting is inconsistency in the implementation of the guidelines. Specialist inpatient facilities with highly structured programmes and a high level of staff training are able to maintain consistent responding far in excess of what can be achieved in non-residential outpatient or day patient programmes. Wood (1988) discussed the difficulties of implementing behaviour management approaches within a day hospital setting, and the need to involve family members to ensure consistency and improve generalisation. A key factor is that of education and training for families (see Chapter 8) but in reality in a community setting it is not often straightforward to involve the family or partner in rehabilitation on a regular basis. Many partners have by this stage returned to work after a prolonged absence and are reluctant to take additional time off. There may be small children in the household and limited access to child care. In practice, many community rehabilitation programmes operate primarily with the patient directly but with some information sharing and involvement of the partner. In the following two examples the strengths and limitations of this essentially pragmatic approach are illustrated.

Michael

Michael was a 34-year-old man who had suffered a severe brain injury in a road traffic accident a year before. At the time of assessment Michael and his partner Helen had received little advice or support about the brain injury. Their main concern related to Michael's poor temper control, particularly as they had an 18-month-old son, Sam, and felt unable to leave him with Michael. Since injury Michael had become more irritable, and subject to what they described as sudden and uncontrollable fits of anger.

Prior to the accident Michael had been working long shifts as a factory worker. He had been weight training five times a week. Helen had also worked, up until the birth of their child and had intended to return to work, although this had not happened because of Michael's accident. During the post-accident period they had developed a number of strategies to help alleviate the stress at home. For example, Helen would sometimes send Michael out of the house if she thought he was becoming agitated, or would go out herself taking Sam with her.

Neuropsychological assessment identified that Michael had made a reasonably good cognitive recovery, scoring within the average range on tests of problem solving and speed of performance. He had some acquired difficulties with reading and writing. On memory testing he was able to perform reasonably well at immediate recall but lost track of information over a delay. He benefited from the repetition of information, with a similar pattern being shown for both verbal and non-verbal information. The test results were consistent with the reports from home, where Michael could, with some prompting and repetition, cope with most day-to-day memory tasks.

Michael described himself as "hyped up" all the time. He tried to use physical activity to release tension but was limited by some residual balance problems and by severe facial pain that was increased by physical exertion. He was acutely aware of what he perceived as his change in status within the household and disliked being dependent on those around him financially, emotionally, and practically. After some initial work on his head pain and physical problems to give him an immediate sense of achievement and control of his progress, a more structured approach to managing his temper control was attempted.

Recording information.   Michael was keen to try whatever was suggested, but his reading and writing difficulties limited the use that could be made of recording sheets. It was also noted that although Michael did not have severe memory deficits, he was more likely to remember to complete a recording chart if it could be attached to a recognisable or familiar event. At this time Michael was using a specific diet for his weight training which involved six regular meals per day at set times, and it was agreed therefore to record the level of anger he felt at each of these intervals over the following week. It was also suggested that if

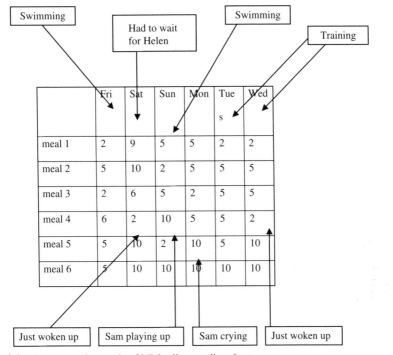

FIG. 6.1   An annotated example of Michael's recording sheet.

he could think of any explanation for "high" or "low" scores it would be useful to know this, although this was not over-emphasised at this stage (see Figure 6.1).

The scoring system (1–10) was worked out with Michael, through discussion during the session. He defined a score of 10 as being "*out of my head*" and a score of 1 as being "*calm*" although he did not think he would use a low score at all. What was apparent from the initial recording was that there were things that helped Michael to relax (sleeping, swimming, training) and that other things resulted in loss of temper (waiting, Sam making a noise). It was also noticeable that there were more high scores in the latter part of the day, indicating that fatigue was a significant component.

Michael's willingness and ability to annotate the recording chart suggested that he would respond well to a more cognitive-behavioural approach to controlling his anger, particularly if the programme related directly to Michael's own experiences using his own words where possible. This was also thought more likely to increase any carryover to the home environment. A visual representation of Michael's anger was developed to help him focus on the process by which his mood changed (Figure 6.2).

Further recordings were made on a weekly basis to identify incidents that could then be discussed in sessions (see Table 6.1). Discussion in the session

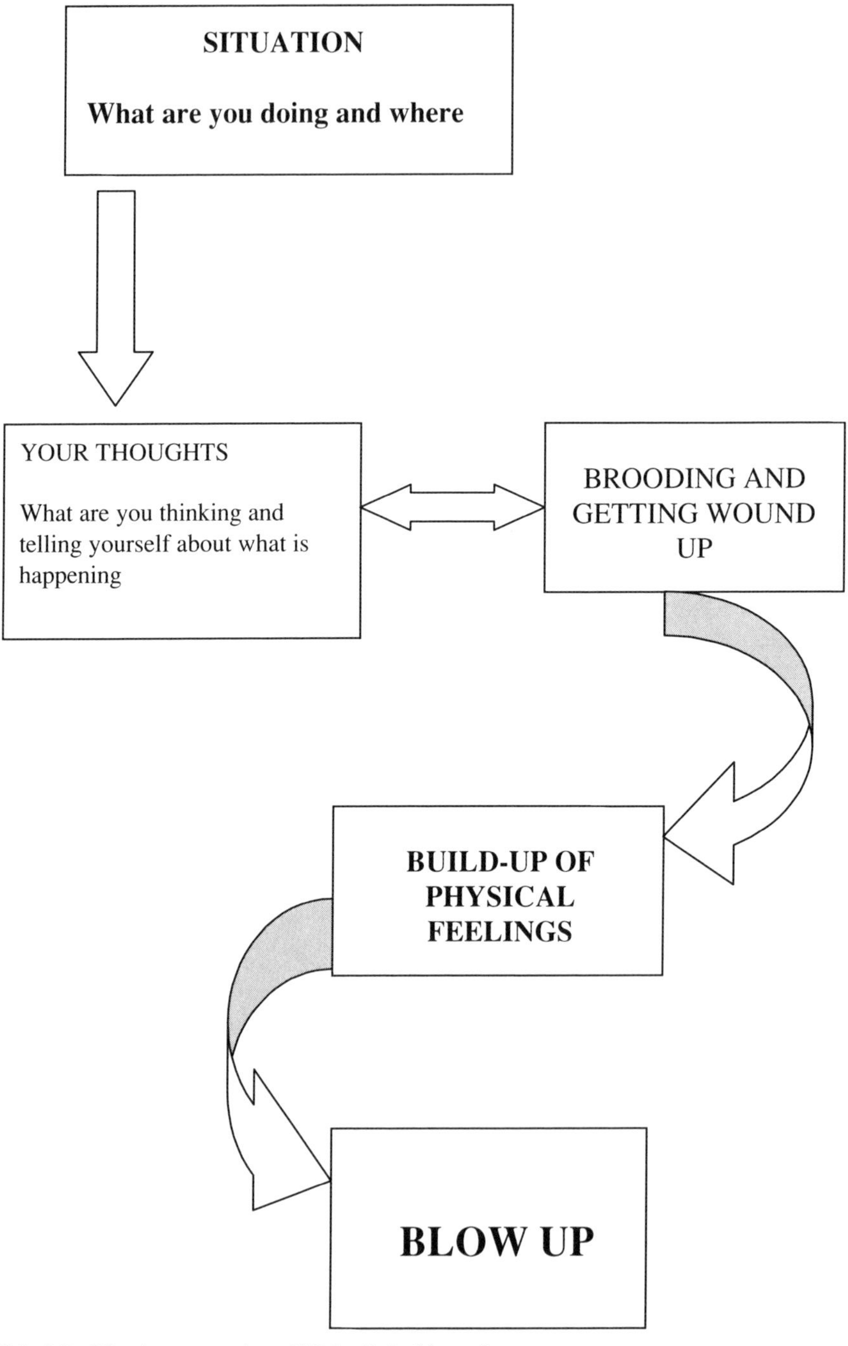

FIG. 6.2 Visual representation of Michael's build-up of anger.

TABLE 6.1
Michael's recording sheet of specific incidents, and their antecedents,
behaviours, and outcomes recorded

THINGS THAT IRRITATE OR UPSET ME

Date/time	Situation where/who	What I did	How angry? 1–10	Outcome
Monday morning	Friend and kids visited	Went upstairs away from kids—knocked stuffing out of bed	8 or 9	Helen came and found me. She got rid of them. Then I got on with the morning
Wednesday morning	Sam/sat in car waiting for Helen	Punch bag for 15 minutes, knocked stuffing out of it until hand could not stand any more	12	F . . . ed but felt great

following these recordings focused on the second incident described in Table 6.1. Michael was able to identify three things that might have helped:

(i)   Getting out of the car before getting wound up.
(ii) Going with Helen, helping her out.
(iii) Even if he had remained in the car initially, he could have got out to cool down once he was annoyed.

Michael tried "not staying in the car" the following week which worked, but he was determined not to be defeated by his temper and set out to find another way round this problem. He eventually identified an alternative activity, playing with Sam, rather than waiting for him to get bored. This alternative turned out to be very successful.

Michael's temper control was also linked to his other cognitive problems, as demonstrated in the following example based on an incident at home when he attempted to set the new video cassette recorder. This required Michael to read the instructions and carry out the task. He attempted to do this while Sam was eating his tea in the same room and with the family pets also milling around in the small front room. Michael became angry and lost his temper, aiming his aggression at the dogs. Discussion of the incident identified this as a high-risk situation. Michael's thinking included self-criticism ("daft idiot—it's only six wires") as well as comparison with himself pre-injury ("I used to be able to do this"). These thoughts went round in his head, causing him to become more wound up and agitated. Sam's presence playing around with his food "would not normally bother me", but on this occasion it did, resulting in a major "blow out".

Michael was then able to come up with alternative strategies for that occasion such as moving away from Sam or not setting the video and asking Helen to do it, although he did not feel that the second option was realistic as he did not want to leave everything difficult to Helen. He was able to stand back and recognise that he had given himself a hard time about his inability to achieve the task and that this had caused more tension. Reading complex instructions was a "high-demand" task for Michael, and one that had not been worked on in therapy. Reading for leisure (body-building magazines) had been explored, but not reading for understanding, where each sentence of information had to be absorbed and subsequent information considered in relation to this. Following this incident some further work on reading was incorporated into his programme.

After six sessions of discussion of incidents a summary was put together incorporating information from the sessions, and using, as far as possible, examples and quotations from Michael's own experiences. This summary was shared with Michael's partner, Helen, and her support was a major factor in the success of this programme. Making time to talk with Helen about how the situation appeared from her point of view was an important part of the programme. Most of the contact was by telephone on a weekly basis and three were regular 3-monthly reviews. Her initial response to the recording system had been cautious as she was unsure of the benefits. However she found the visual representation of the sequence of events helpful as an explanation of why things got out of control, and she was also able to see how the strategies that she had developed for herself could be seen as "positive coping". At times she had felt that leaving the situation, or sending Michael out had been a sign of weakness, of running away from the problem, even though it had calmed things down. Although the emphasis was on helping Michael to change what happened, her cooperation and understanding were crucial. Direct input on temper control was discontinued at this stage but Michael remained within the service for a further period of time, working on other problems. The situation at home was kept under review and will be returned to again later in this chapter.

Robert

In the second case example there were similar problems with child care and distance from the rehabilitation facility, which limited the contact between staff and the wider family. In this example this proved to be a major impediment to progress and greater effort was made to engage the partner more actively in the rehabilitation programme.

Robert was a 26-year-old man who had been injured in a motorbike accident 8 months prior to assessment. He sustained a skull fracture and an extradural haematoma, which was surgically evacuated on two occasions. He also fractured his left femur and left clavicle. He remained in hospital for approximately 3 weeks and was discharged home.

At the time of assessment Robert was living with his wife Tracy and two children aged 3 years and 18 months. He was spending his days sitting at home listening to music or watching television. He complained of feeling bored and at the same time he complained of frustration because he could not complete previously routine tasks. He acknowledged that he became "grumpy" when bored and that he lost his temper easily. The family situation was complicated by the fact that prior to the accident Robert and Tracy had recently separated. Robert had left the family home several days before the accident had occurred, and had gone to live with his parents. It was a close-knit community with a strong sense of family, and after the accident Tracy decided to remain involved.

Assessment identified significant cognitive problems. Robert had an acquired reading disorder, affecting his ability to identify single letters accurately and he struggled to decipher words, especially those with irregular spellings. He had a limited working memory capacity and performed poorly on both verbal and visual memory tasks. Perceptual problems were also demonstrated on initial testing, but on further investigation were found to be secondary to poor organisation and planning skills. He also had some continuing problems with pain from his orthopaedic fixation, and his gait was abnormal.

The initial treatment programme focused on helping Robert to regain basic functional independence within the home, with a secondary emphasis on reading skills as a basis for the use of a broader range of memory aids and planning skills. However, in view of the continuing reports of poor temper control within the home environment it was agreed to try and gain further information and develop a structured intervention if appropriate.

Recording information. In Robert's case there were three phases.

Phase 1: As a result of preliminary discussions with Robert it did appear that there were certain flash points in the home situation, for example when his older child returned home from school and wanted to play. Robert's reading and writing had improved to the point where he was capable of some recording of information, at least sufficient to form a basis for discussion. An attempt was therefore made to record events over the period of a week, in order to explore the pattern in more detail, but Robert could not comply with this. He wanted to talk about pre-injury problems and how angry he felt about the marital situation at that time. He found it difficult to let go of his anger, or to see how anything could be done to change or improve the situation.

Phase 2: An attempt was made to work with Robert and Tracy together on a problem-solving approach. Initial groundwork had indicated that Tracy was unwilling to engage in a discussion about their relationship, but she did produce a written list of situations within the home that precipitated angry scenes:

(1) Hospital transport delays.
(2) Excessive fatigue, e.g., if he had been to town and tried to do some gardening.
(3) Getting up in a bad mood and staying that way all day.
(4) Sudden changes in mood when Tracy has responded in a similar vein.
(5) Not doing things around the house even when asked several times.

Although most outbursts were described as verbal aggression, at least one serious incident in which Robert was said to have threatened Tracy with a knife was reported. Neither Robert nor Tracy were prepared to address this incident in any detail and were keen to play it down. They wanted to discuss the more routine incidents that were more frequent and to them more disturbing. However neither of them was able to commit to a systematic analysis of the pattern or cause of the incidents, so the approach taken was based on general principles:

(1) to encourage Robert to pace his activities appropriately to reduce fatigue;
(2) to encourage an appropriate sleep habit;
(3) to define the range and frequency of household tasks that Robert could reasonably complete;
(4) to develop memory systems to minimise the risk of arguments resulting from memory failures.

These rehabilitation goals were an extension of the initial treatment plan but with a secondary aim of attempting to reduce tension within the home environment. There was some limited success in all areas, with the relationship improving to the point where Robert and Tracy were able to plan a number of social outings together without the children. In spite of these outward signs of progress there was little sense that either Robert or Tracy had internalised the general principles or would be able to apply them to future situations without ongoing support.

Phase 3: With the majority of his rehabilitation goals achieved and discharge being planned, Robert began talking again about the problems of poor temper control. He could acknowledge the progress he had made in other areas but felt frustrated at the continuing loss of temper. He was concerned by the amount of shouting he was doing at home, and the effect this was having on his children. A further attempt was made therefore to explore strategies for anger management.

By this stage Robert was able to be relatively articulate in discussion about the causes of his loss of temper. In particular he described the daily frustrations that arise from two small children asking repetitively for attention. He said that he tended to react first and then think of a more reasonable solution. His reaction was not predictable, being dependent on his mood, and he could see

TABLE 6.2
Robert's recording sheet for episodes of aggression, with antecendents,
behaviours, and outcomes recorded

THINGS THAT IRRITATE OR UPSET ME

Date/time	Situation where/who	What I did	How angry? 1–10	Outcome
Early hours 12.00 am	Stewart in bed	Shouted, got angry	5	Made him worse, got up, made me ratty next day
Early hours	Stewart in bed	Thought about it, didn't shout	1 or 2	He felt better, slept rest of night

that the children were often frightened of him. The focus on his children was reflected in the limited amount of recording that Robert managed to produce (see Table 6.2).

Robert could also understand the concept of thinking about alternative strategies, and attempting to implement them. For example, he could recognise that he was better at dealing with naughty behaviour by the children if they were playing at some distance from him. This gave him time to stop and think, and might result in him sending them to their bedroom rather than hitting them. Another example related to the children's mealtimes, which had developed into an ongoing battle. Again, Robert could come up with a number of potential solutions, and, because it was a regular occurrence, he was able to implement some of the strategies with obvious good effect.

What Robert was unable to achieve was the ability to recognise the principles underlying his temper control. He could, with time and encouragement, reflect on individual occurrences. He could not generalise from one situation to the next. He was aware that Tracy often intervened to slow him down and prevent an angry interaction with the children, but could not see that there might also be examples in their own relationship where "taking time to think" could have prevented an argument. Unfortunately Tracy's involvement in these discussions was minimal. She was offered opportunities to discuss the situation and the difficulties at times and locations that were more convenient for her, but she did not make use of these openings. While there were clearly a number of potential explanations for her lack of involvement, there is no doubt that it did limit the effectiveness of such a community-based programme. The option of removing Robert from the family home, for example for inpatient rehabilitation, was not considered viable. The presenting problems were based in the family environment and the rationale for treatment needed to include engaging with the family. Although ultimately this was not in itself successful, it is not clear that addressing Robert's difficulties in isolation from his family would have been more successful.

Episodic dyscontrol

A particularly disruptive and distressing form of post-traumatic aggression is the explosive, often dramatic and disruptive, but usually brief outbursts that result from episodic dyscontrol syndrome. This problem typically appears some months after injury, although it may be delayed for several years. It has many similarities with epilepsy (delayed onset, paroxysmal pattern, brief duration, dysthymic after effects, and responsiveness to anticonvulsant drugs). Episodic dyscontrol syndrome following brain injury has been documented in the literature (Eames, 1988), and is most clearly associated with medial temporal lesions affecting the limbic structures. These bursts of violent aggression are usually unprovoked, poorly controlled, and short-lived. They are also usually followed by emotional distress and remorse, and may be out of character with behaviour seen between outbursts. The behaviours exhibited can be extreme—for example, one patient complained that he had "gone through two doors in his house" but could not remember having done so. He described it afterwards with humour, with the doors resembling something out of a cartoon, but he was clearly frightened by what he had done and by his inability to remember having done it.

Although this syndrome is deemed rare, Eames, Haffey, and Cope (1990) found that at least a third of the individuals attending a routine head-injury follow-up clinic showed evidence of the disorder. Where the aggression is thought to be epileptogenic in origin behavioural approaches are rarely sufficient, and treatment with appropriate medication is recommended.

The problems created by episodic dyscontrol were demonstrated subsequently at a follow-up visit to Michael and Helen 12 months after the completion of the anger-management programme. At this review appointment a year after the anger-management work the approach was still described as beneficial by both Michael and Helen, but there was an additional sense of crisis. There had been a recent incident where Michael had lost control and had found himself with his hands around Helen's throat before he realised what was happening. Both of them were extremely concerned, particularly about the effect this might have on Sam who had witnessed the incident. Further discussion identified that there had been a number of factors that had raised the general level of tension in the household. For example, as a result of the breakdown of their car Michael had not been able to get to his fitness training and Helen had also had to limit her activities outside the home. In addition they had both been worried by the financial pressures of repairing the car. With time to reflect on what had happened they felt that these additional pressures were the probable cause of the recent incident, but they described the continuing strain of living with the potential for loss of control. However hard they tried they could not run their lives completely in accordance with what Michael required to retain control. They described it as being like "living with a volcano". Michael was referred for a further opinion and prescribed Tegretol, which reduced the underlying tension to a point where the cognitive-behavioural strategies could be effective.

Although it is good practice to use a less invasive intervention first, clinicians should be aware of the ethical considerations associated with some behavioural interventions and should be prepared to consider the potential benefits of other approaches such as medication in treating behavioural disorders.

BEHAVIOURAL MANAGEMENT OF DISINHIBITED BEHAVIOUR

Disinhibited behaviour is relatively common after brain injury, but is often neglected other than when it is extreme in its manifestations. A broad spectrum of impulsivity or inappropriate social and sexual behaviours may be found particularly in patients with frontal lobe injury. Sexual disinhibition, which can take a verbal form of obscene comments or a physical form ranging from unwelcome touching to physical assault, can result in admission to specialist units for treatment. Socially disinhibited behaviours can range from extremes of repetitive screaming or excessive use of behaviours such as nose picking, throat clearing, or spitting, through to more subtle questions of social judgement. At this end of the spectrum it can be difficult to define the problem or develop a treatment approach, whereas at the other extreme this is less of an issue.

In many cases the inappropriateness of the behaviour is all too obvious within any setting. A common example within inpatient services and on occasions within the home environment is where the patient shouts repeatedly and without ceasing, in order to gain attention. This type of behaviour has been successfully addressed by satiation through negative practice (see Alderman, 1991, for a more detailed description) and by a behavioural points systems (Burke & Lewis, 1986). In this study the behaviours targeted were loud verbal outbursts, interruptions, and nonsensical talk. The study used a mixture of reinforcement, using items chosen from the menu or activities that the client enjoyed and which were easily deliverable, and a points card with the target behaviours written out together with the criteria for correct performance. The client received a point if he performed the target behaviour correctly within each 4-minute interval. A zero was recorded if he demonstrated incorrect usage of the skill at any time during the interval. If the client met the points criteria he could choose an item from the reinforcement menu. Treatment was given during meal periods in a multiple baseline design across the three behaviours. The client ate at a table with the therapist and no more than four staff or clients not involved in the training.

Two of the behaviours, verbal outbursts and interruptions, were more responsive to treatment than nonsensical talk, which remained at a dysfunctionally high rate. In general, nonsensical comments appeared to be associated with unstructured social interactions, and were at times attributable to uncontrolled variation in the number of spontaneous interactions directed at the client by others in the dining room. This study, while demonstrating clear benefits, does illustrate some of the difficulties of treating disinhibited behaviour in more realistic settings. The authors point out that nonsensical talk had been reinforced in the past with attention given by family and staff, and suggest that to achieve a further reduction in this behaviour the treatment programme would need shorter time intervals for the delivery of feedback and reinforcement, additional social skills training to teach appropriate alternative responses, and staff training to promote consistency in reinforcing appropriate verbalisations and extinguishing nonsensical comments. This study did look at generalisation of treatment effects beyond the treatment setting by collecting data on the target behaviours in informal restaurants in the community. They did find some evidence for skill generalisation to other settings, with data from a 2-week follow-up showing that all target behaviours had reduced to zero levels.

For many brain-injured patients with intact speech ability, it is their poor conversational skills that contribute to their inappropriate behaviour in social situations and which contribute to the social isolation of many of them and their families. Talking too much, repeating the same topic or question, using inappropriate language for particular situations, being unable to take turns in a conversation, are all patterns of communication that are difficult to live with and yet are relatively common after brain injury. There have been a small number of studies that have looked at modifying conversation skills. (Braunling-McMorrow, 1994; Burke & Lewis, 1986; Gajar, Schloss, Schloss, & Thompson, 1984; Lewis, Nelson, Nelson, & Reusink, 1988; Schloss, Thompson, Gajar, & Schloss, 1985). Gajar et al., for example, gave feedback in the form of a cue light and prompts to self-monitor to enhance conversational skills in adolescents with traumatic brain injury. Some generalisation was noted in a group that was less structured yet very similar to an initial training group. Another study (Lewis et al., 1988) targeted socially inappropriate verbalisations in an adult with traumatic brain injury. Three types of feedback—attention and interest, systematic ignoring, and verbal correction—were administered during naturally occurring social interactions. The results indicated that the correction feedback was most effective in reducing inappropriate talk, while the attention and interest feedback increased the frequency of the targeted behaviour.

It is usually the frequency and quality of the behaviour that results in it being described as inappropriate. For example, the use of swear words is not inappropriate in all contexts and by all people, but excessive swearing can be. The use of verbal threats, suggestive sexual comments, or over-familiar questions and remarks can make staff or family and friends feel uncomfortable. Where the changes are subtle they can be difficult to define or describe. Staff and family are often reluctant to be seen to be imposing their own standards on the brain-injured individual, for example where a joke went "a bit too far" or where the patient "said what we all thought but none of the rest of us would actually say it".

Where the patient is interacting with non-specialist services there may be a lack of understanding of the role of the injury in the behaviour, as was illustrated when one patient, Brian, began attending a local further education college. Brian had been injured in a road traffic accident when he was 16. He suffered a severe head injury and was unconscious for over a month. At a year post-injury he was discharged from hospital with continuing problems with language, both dysarthria and dysphasia, concentration and memory difficulties, impulsive behaviour, poor temper control, and continuing physical difficulties. He attended outpatient rehabilitation for a further year during which time he made slow progress, as his cognitive deficits affected his ability to make the physical gains he saw as desirable. Brian moved on to attend a slow-stream computing course at the local college. Within this more open environment Brian's sexually inappropriate comments and touching behaviour, which had been apparent but controlled within the rehabilitation centre, became more of an issue. The main problem was that, being unfamiliar with the nature of brain injury, the staff at the college were attributing to Brian a greater degree of control of his behaviour than in fact he was able to exert. They had noticed that Brian did not make inappropriate comments to all members of staff, and reasoned that if he could control it sometimes then he should be able to control it at all times. More detailed analysis of the type of incidents revealed that Brian was approaching young blonde females, or new and unconfident members of staff. If he received an ambivalent response—a giggle or a comment back—he would continue and return later.

Intervention consisted of a staff training session, backed up by written material, to explain the nature of brain injury and how it had affected Brian in particular. It emphasised the problems with memory, stating clearly that the staff could not rely on Brian remembering information the same day or the next day, giving advice about how to present information, the value of writing it down, and keeping a copy to avoid arguments. It went on to talk more directly about Brian's impulsiveness and his varying control over his inappropriate comments and touching (see Table 6.3).

A follow-up meeting after a month identified that the concern about the behaviour had reduced, although there were still a number of incidents. Awareness of the likelihood of staff turnover and the problems of ensuring that information was passed on to new members was discussed, with no easy solutions identified. However, 12 months on, Brian was still attending college and had not been excluded as originally suggested.

When patients are being treated on an outpatient basis or in community settings these types of conversational problems can be difficult to treat because of the lack of control over the environment and the difficulty in gaining sufficient information about the patterns of interaction. The effects of other cognitive problems can exacerbate the treatment problems as demonstrated in the treatment programme designed for Stephen, a 48-year-old bricklayer, who suffered a severe head injury in a fall from a roof. On assessment a year post-injury he was

TABLE 6.3

Information sheet for staff to help them understand Brian's brain injury and its effects on his behaviour

---

Brian—the effect of his brain injury on his behaviour

Brian will act impulsively. This is also a direct consequence of his brain injury. He will speak and act without thinking. This does not mean that he cannot understand when he does something that is unacceptable, but it does mean that the signals that a set of behaviours is unacceptable have to be sufficiently clear and strong so that they can overcome a strong impulse. This is why he can control his inappropriate sexual comments and touching with known staff members or with people who present as firm and standing for "no nonsense" but the impulse to act remains present.

(1) Be explicit about what constitutes unacceptable behaviour in particular situations.
(2) Be consistent in responding to it.
(3) Give a clear and unambiguous response.

---

repetitive in questioning, interrupted inappropriately, changed topic frequently, and apologised excessively. He had severe deficits in all areas of executive functioning, with poor insight into his current problems and deficits in memory and reasoning. However it was his communication style that was identified by his wife and family as being the greatest cause of strain. He would invariably bring the conversation round to one of a restricted range of topics such as swearing, lying, people he disliked, religion, the building trade, and football coaching. He would frequently shift topic without an appropriate signal to the hearer, which his family described as "not keeping to the point" such that they could not follow him.

The first stage of treatment was to try and raise Stephen's awareness of the patterns of communication he was using and to give him structured opportunities to alter these patterns. He was asked to describe procedures and narratives while "keeping to the point" and was given the opportunity to reflect on his performance via video and audio feedback and by discussion with the therapist. It rapidly became clear that Stephen could not recognise any but the most blatant shifts of topic in his own or others' output after the event, and could not monitor topic shift as it happened. The focus of therapy moved to structuring Stephen's communication without requiring him to monitor the process. A list of prescribed topics was agreed with his family and recorded in his personal organiser. Each time Stephen introduced one of these topics within the outpatient unit he was referred to the list of "prohibited" subjects in the book.

Initially, this approach met with some success, as Stephen came to start a topic and would say, "I'm not supposed to talk about that, am I?", but it became clear that the breadth of the subjects made it difficult to pin down exactly what he should and should not talk about. Stephen did not have the cognitive ability to judge when it was actually appropriate to discuss, for example, football. The programme therefore transferred to the home environment where his wife and daughters, who had been involved in discussions from the beginning of the programme, were asked to take a more active role. They agreed to a procedure whereby at the first mention of the topic in question the listener would say to Stephen, "You've agreed not to talk about that", and would leave the room for 2 minutes. Although this was difficult for family members to achieve, the strategy worked and the behaviour decreased rapidly. The approach was subsequently applied to other topics, and Stephen was also given some "safe" questions that he could ask new visitors to the house, when his conversational skills appeared to be at their most vulnerable.

BEHAVIOURAL MANAGEMENT OF SEXUAL PROBLEMS FOLLOWING BRAIN INJURY

As patients emerge from coma and low awareness states, many patients will engage in genital fondling and masturbation. The behavioural issue here is usually the semi-public nature of the actions. In most cases intervention is in the form of ensuring privacy and in redirecting the patient's attention to alternative activities when necessary.

In the post-acute and early rehabilitation phases, sexually disinhibited behaviours are often secondary to continuing confusion and disorientation. The individual may be unaware of the behaviour or of its effects. Clear feedback stating that the behaviour is inappropriate in this situation is usually sufficient.

Longer-term studies of sexuality following traumatic brain injury have focused primarily on changes in sex drive and sexual behaviour. Although brain injury can result in either a loss of sex drive or increased sexual desire, hyposexuality is reported more widely than hypersexuality (Kreutzer & Zasler, 1989). Significant changes in sexual behaviour are widely reported, and in most instances these are of a negative nature. Kreutzer and Zasler found that 57% of respondents indicated a diminished ability to maintain an erection, and a third of the sample reported greater difficulty in achieving an orgasm. They also found that 62% of subjects reported diminished frequency of sexual intercourse, with only one person indicating an increase in frequency of intercourse.

In spite of the reported frequency of change in sexual behaviour following TBI, in many instances sexual issues are frequently not discussed during rehabilitation. Prior to intervention it is important to carry out a comprehensive assessment covering the range of organic causes (endocrine dysfunction, sensori-motor problems, cognitive and behavioural dysfunction, changes in libido, etc.) as well as considering the emotional and relationship problems and other stresses that may be affecting performance. For a detailed account of the causes, nature, and management of sexual problems associated with traumatic brain injury there are two useful review articles (Horn & Zasler, 1990; Zasler & Horn, 1990). Zasler and Horn emphasise the need to distinguish hypersexuality, thought to be associated with limbic dysfunction, from disinhibition. Rehabilitation staff and families also need to recognise the difference between expressions of sexual frustration and sexual disinhibition.

Where the disinhibited behaviour continues and is sufficient to interfere with ongoing rehabilitation or with attempts to move the individual to a community setting, behavioural management approaches can be effective. Zencius, Wesolowski, Burke, and Hough (1990) presented three case studies of the use of a behavioural framework to decrease hypersexual behaviour. In the first example, Kathy, a 19-year-old woman with cognitive, physical, and behavioural deficits, demonstrated physical and verbal aggression and disinhibited sexual behaviour. Sexual activity was defined as touching or sitting within 1 foot of a member of the opposite sex. After 7 days of baseline data collection, scheduled feedback was given to Kathy every half hour regarding her interactions with males for 25 days, then this decreased to one session per evening. This continued for a further 2 months, following which Kathy was transferred to a community placement, where feedback continued twice a week. It is not clear, however, how this feedback was maintained and whether it was considered necessary to continue to provide feedback, albeit in a limited form for the foreseeable future.

In the second case, Jack, a 32-year-old man, who had been unconscious for 24 hours with frontal oedema seen on the CT scan, recovered physically, but became impulsive, began to abuse alcohol, showed poor judgement, and demonstrated inappropriate sexual behaviour, i.e., exposing himself, resulting in arrest, followed by admission to a rehabilitation facility. Exhibitionism was the target behaviour, with two episodes during the first week at the rehabilitation facility, and only one incident in 24 weeks once the treatment package was implemented. Treatment involved a detailed interview of Jack's urges, feelings, and fantasies before and during an act of exhibitionism. He was provided with a self-monitoring notebook to record all urges and feelings. During the situations when Jack had the urge to expose himself, he was told to record the urge in the notebook and then to masturbate to fantasies of situations presented in a dating skills training class. Unfortunately no follow-up data were presented and it is not known whether Jack went on to re-offend. What this case does illustrate is how vulnerable many of these patients can become if left unsupervised or unmonitored.

The third case report is that of Gary, 24 years old, with severe short-term memory deficits. He presented as verbally abusive to staff and peers, impulsive, and invasive of others' personal space. Staff complained that Gary would inappropriately touch staff and peers, frequently giving back rubs and kissing females' hands, both of which were used as the dependent measure. Treatment consisted of allowing Gary to rub backs during a scheduled relaxation class, while on any occasions outside the class that he attempted to touch people, he was reminded that back rubs were to be given only during the relaxation class.

Again the success of the programme is described in relation to the back rubbing, but it is not made clear whether this generalised to the inappropriate kissing of hands.

Turner, Green, and Braunling-McMorrow (1990) treated a 21-year-old brain-injured man who exhibited verbal disinhibition, both suggestive sexual comments and personal comments/questions to strangers, and physical behaviours such as inappropriate touching. He also made verbally aggressive comments (swearing, threats, etc.) and showed some physical aggression (shaking fist or cane, hitting, and shoving). Turner et al. used a multiple baseline design across three settings —clinical sessions, group house, and community activity sessions—that used differential reinforcement of low rates of inappropriate behaviour (DRL), along with differential reinforcement of other behaviour. The DRL component of the intervention allowed for the establishment of an initial criterion rate that was relatively easy for the participant to attain, so the reinforcing contingencies were easily established. If the participant exhibited frequencies of behaviours in the combined verbal and physical categories that were at or below specified criteria for a specified time period, he was awarded points towards a weekly goal. The criterion was lowered gradually in successive intervention phases, ensuring a high rate of reinforcement throughout the intervention until the problematic behaviours were occurring at acceptably low rates. Although there was no systematic evaluation of the generalisation of the intervention, anecdotal reports from family members suggest that the participant did handle a variety of social situations appropriately, and 2 months after the intervention began, the rates of behaviour in both categories had decreased to the point where the participant could move to a more independent living facility.

McMillan et al. (1990) also described a behavioural management programme to control hypersexuality, in this instance following herpes simplex encephalitis. The programme used edible reinforcers and verbal reprimands. The behaviour was managed in supervised environments allowing for discharge into the community with progress maintained. It was noted however that the problems resurfaced if supervision was removed.

In many cases it is when the supervision is removed or unavailable that problems re-occur. Unless a package of care is established that provides the type of prompting or supervision required, the individual with a brain injury will be vulnerable to exploitation, which is unfortunately what happened to Kelly. She was 17 years old when she was assaulted by her boyfriend, sustaining a severe brain injury. She was unconscious for approximately 7 weeks. She made a good physical recovery although she had a slight weakness of the left side, causing her to drag her foot when tired. On assessment 7 years post-injury she had problems with acquiring, retaining, and recalling verbally presented material. She was unable to give reliable information about events on a day-to-day basis. She was highly distractible. She showed an impaired ability to make reflective judgements and impairment in social appropriateness. She showed some insight into her problems of poor temper control, restlessness, and the fact that she was unconcerned about how others felt about her behaviour, but had a strong tendency to underestimate the extent of these and other difficulties and was unrealistic about the future.

In the intervening years since injury Kelly had been living primarily with her parents, both of whom worked. At an early stage Kelly had been through a rehabilitation programme that had successfully placed her in sheltered employment. Her father was at that time able to take her to work and collect her again. Subsequently his own work pattern changed and he was no longer able to do this. Kelly proved to be unable to get herself to work, and regularly diverted to the local pub or club. Here she would drink excessively and had a series of sexual encounters with people whose names she could not remember. Although her parents attempted to keep a close watch on her, and rescued her from many potentially difficult situations, she went missing for days at a time, often returning with bruises on her arms and legs, and unable to give any account of where she had been. As Kelly was over 18 years old she was deemed to be legally an adult and therefore the local police were unable to assist her parents in finding her, although on many occasions they did actually do so. On superficial meeting Kelly looked and sounded "normal" and she was therefore attributed a level of control over her behaviour that she did not have. She could articulate what would be sensible or risky behaviour if in certain situations. She could say, for example, that it would be foolish to go off with a man that she had just met, and would say that she would never do that. Unfortunately there was ample evidence to demonstrate that she was unable to act on what she could say. Kelly's vulnerability was such that she was persuaded to engage in illegal sexual activities including pornographic videos. Although she denied any recollection of this, there was in this instance evidence of her involvement.

Attempts were made to provide an appropriate placement for Kelly, but she resisted any suggestion of a residential assessment or placement, and continued to abscond regularly, returning to her usual pattern of alcohol and sexual activity. Eventually a package of care was established that involved the recruitment of age-appropriate carers who would be with Kelly on a shift basis throughout her waking day. The carers acted as Kelly's "frontal lobes" and prevented her getting into situations that provoked her sexual activity. They would divert Kelly from potentially difficult situations by distracting her attention. They planned a range of activities and offered Kelly a limited choice. Together they were able to decorate and move into separate accommodation, with Kelly being more closely involved in domestic activities. Tight control was kept over the financial arrangements, and Kelly was required to budget for her alcohol consumption. The greater level of general activity also served to reduce the amount of time Kelly spent in the pub. With this level of supervision, no further incidents of sexual exploitation occurred by a 2-year follow-up interview, and Kelly's general range of socially appropriate behaviours had increased.

SUMMARY

Behavioural management approaches have become the treatment of choice for aggressive behaviour following brain injury. They are sufficiently flexible to be applicable in a range of settings, although the need for consistency and clear feedback is often difficult to achieve in a more community-based setting.

Disinhibited behaviour can be a major factor in failure to integrate back into community settings. A combination of behavioural and cognitive approaches can be used to enable family members and the person with the brain injury to maintain some control over such behaviours, although in more extreme cases such packages can be expensive to set up and run. In addition it is not always appropriate for family members to be required to take on the additional strain of managing such behaviour. Consideration should be given to the emotional as well as the practical problems of enabling family members or paid carers to implement behaviour regimens within a home setting.

CHAPTER 7

Behavioural approaches to cooperation with treatment: The effects of mood, insight, and motivation

Changes in mood, lack of insight, and poor motivation are common problems within brain-injury rehabilitation and have a significant effect on level of cooperation with rehabilitation programmes and on their success.

Non-cooperation with treatment can be an "active" process involving aggression or overt refusal. Where aggression is the primary response, this was considered in more detail in Chapter 6. More commonly however, non-cooperation takes a "passive" form of failure to attend sessions, or not participating fully in sessions. There are many reasons why a person with a brain injury may lack motivation or not comply with a treatment programme. First, their cognitive problems may be such that they cannot remember what is expected of them, or they may be unable to organise themselves to respond to a specific request (Zencius, Wesolowski, Burke, & McQuaide, 1989). Second, the person with the brain injury may struggle to initiate activities successfully. Third, they may lack insight into their problems, which is one of the greatest challenges to success in rehabilitation. Fourth, emotional responses such as low mood and anxiety, or learned responses such as learned helplessness or avoidance, may prevent an individual engaging in treatment (Feinstein, 1999). Fifth, the individual's level of fatigue may reduce their ability to participate fully, and activities and therapy programmes must be structured to give periods of rest as required. Finally there is a general reduction in arousal levels that some patients experience which significantly affects their ability to participate in activities (Andersson, Gundersen, & Finset, 1999) and which may be amenable to pharmacological interventions. A good behavioural analysis is crucial to assist in determining which are the important factors in each case.

In this chapter the management of mood, insight, and motivation will be considered, particularly in relation to maximising attendance or cooperation with treatment programmes and care regimes. The longer-term consequences of non-cooperation and the issues of consent to treatment and support for vulnerable adults will also be addressed.

BEHAVIOURAL MANAGEMENT OF MOOD DISORDERS

Altered emotional control

For many people with brain injury their emotional responses, particularly in the early stages, are not fully under their control. During the period of post traumatic amnesia they are usually confused and unable to make sense of what has happened to them and what is going on around them now. They may be erratic in mood and show exaggerated emotional responses to events in their immediate environment. Some of the inappropriateness of the responses is a consequence of the person's inability to correctly interpret the environment. If the patient is picking up only on certain factors within the conversation or social situation, their emotional response may not actually relate to the topic or event. This can be confusing and upsetting for staff and families who are trying to interact reasonably with the patient. The patient may also be unhappy about their situation, either generally, for example, not wanting to be in hospital, or more specifically, for example, being frustrated at not being able to walk or dress themselves. These negative feelings are often projected onto staff and family.

The most common, and very distressing, change is the unexpected and unpredictable mood changes that affect the way the family and staff react to the individual. In the early stages such mood swings are best managed by a steady calm response from the staff and family. Reacting to the emotion can serve to reinforce the behaviour. In these early stages in particular, the patient's ability to empathise is usually very limited and the individual can appear indifferent to other people's problems. It is not usually effective to try to rationalise the patient's emotions at this stage or to attempt to show them how they are shocking or hurting their family or staff by their language or actions. It is more helpful to model calm, stable, and non-confrontative behaviour.

In contrast with their seeming lack of awareness or concern for the impact of their behaviour on others, people with brain injury can be very sensitive to criticism and failure. The exact nature of the failure or reason for the embarrassment may be difficult for them to identify, as they are often not aware of the direct consequences of their behaviour. As a result they may be surprised and hurt by what seems to them unexpected criticism. It is usually more helpful to reinforce alternative behaviours or to redirect them towards other strategies, for example by saying "Possibly this may work better".

One of the consequences of the general reduction in the effectiveness of an individual's coping skills is that they become more vulnerable to stress. The normal limits of coping and stress tolerance are stretched for everyone by abnormal or extreme events such as death, divorce, or other major life events. When the stress exceeds the ability of the patient to cope, frustration, anger, withdrawal, and mood swings can occur. For someone with a brain injury whose coping strategies are limited, even very minor stresses can be overwhelming. Reducing the demands placed on the individual can stabilise the mood swings to some extent, but this is not always possible to achieve. Stress management approaches can be helpful later in rehabilitation once a greater level of insight has been gained.

Depression and anxiety

As patients progress through rehabilitation and become in many cases increasingly aware of their cognitive, emotional, physical, and behavioural changes, they often experience a "catastrophic reaction" as they struggle to cope with their deficits. With increasing awareness the patient becomes more depressed. By this stage many patients have returned home or to some form of longer-term residential setting after a period of more intensive rehabilitation. Rates of depression following brain injury of up to 55% have been cited (Garske & Thomas, 1992), with rates remaining stable at 6 months to 1 year post-injury (Bowen, Chamberlain, Tennant, Neumann, & Conner, 1999; Bowen, Neumann, Conner, Tennant, & Chamberlain, 1998). There is also some evidence of an increased suicide risk (Teasdale & Engberg, 2001). Increasing self-doubt and a sense of helplessness causes the patient to withdraw, becoming more isolated and depressed. The patient may present in a state of agitated depression, with anxiety, occasional rage, uncooperativeness, and general irritability. Alcohol and drug abuse may become additional problems in an attempt to escape the inability to cope with the world (Sparadeo, Strauss, & Barth, 1990).

Whilst some patients are capable of engaging in a more psychodynamic reinterpretation of their changed roles and sense of self, for many people with brain injury their cognitive deficits limit their ability to deal with more abstract concepts and their memory skills may be such that they struggle to follow a discussion within a session or between sessions. Greater use of written or recorded material is necessary and frequent recapping of significant points is required. The usefulness of metaphor and analogy can be limited, as rigid thinking and difficulty in generalising restrict the patient's ability to use these ways of thinking, but examples from day-to-day practice or from the patient's own experience can be used to build an account of emotions and social interactions that makes sense to that individual. Self-instructional techniques, particularly those based on repetitive practice, can help the patient to internalise the treatment approach. Malec (1984) describes a case in which a deficit of self-monitoring of her own behaviour was thought to be contributing to the patient's tendency to over-generalise her assessment of negative events. Her response to a small failure rapidly became an indication to her that she was "worthless and unable to do anything". The depressive behaviours associated with such cognitions were having a deleterious effect on her marriage. Following a period of training to help her identify inaccurate overgeneralised statements, she began a programme of monitoring and limiting such statements, making use of an index card with a brief explanation of the kinds of statements she was monitoring for herself. She shared this card with her therapists and enlisted their help in calling overgeneralised statements to her attention. Positive events and behaviours were also recorded. She began to identify behaviours in her own repertoire which produced positive outcomes, and this process in itself became rewarding. At follow-up, after discharge from the rehabilitation facility, feedback from the patient and her husband was positive.

In many cases however, the treatment may need to focus on addressing the limitations imposed by the injury rather than on the cognitions surrounding the change in status and role. There needs to be a balance between acknowledging the distress and not reinforcing it by attention. Repeated rehearsal of difficulties without progress or prospect of resolution can in itself perpetuate the distress. Distraction at the time and active approaches to reduce or change the reality of the situation more generally can both be effective ways of maintaining a more positive mood state.

Anxiety disorders may emerge in relation to specific treatments or inter-ventions and are often amenable to behavioural approaches. The behavioural ana-lysis may identify specific cognitive problems that contribute to the individual's fear or anxiety in the situation. The intervention may then consist of altering the way in which the treatment is delivered to avoid precipitating the anxiety or fear (Youngson & Alderman, 1992). At other times anxiety management training, involving relaxation or graded hierarchies can be helpful, although there have been very few studies that address treatment approaches in this area. Lysaght and Bodenheimer (1990) treated stress in four patients using relaxation training, including biofeedback, autogenic exercise, imagery, deep breathing, and home practice. A self-report measurement of physical and psychological functioning documented that improvement was noted and maintained at 4 weeks.

Post traumatic stress disorder

The frequency of post traumatic stress disorder following brain injury is unclear, but it is not thought to be common. McMillan (1996) reported 10 cases out of 312 seen for neuropsychological assessment or for admission to rehabilitation. Warden et al. (1997) examined the case notes of 47 service personnel who had sustained a head injury while on active service. They were unable to identify any cases of PTSD that matched DSM 111R criteria. Williams, Evans, Wilson, and

Needham (2002) found that studies reported rates of PTSD ranging from 1% to 50%. In their particular study, these authors found 18% of participants to have PTSD.

Where the condition is identified, the limited number of published studies suggests that behavioural and cognitive behavioural approaches are appropriate and successful. McMillan (1991) described a behavioural approach to treatment, and McGrath (1997) describes a case report of cognitive behavioural treatment. Miller (1993) reported on both behavioural and psychodynamic approaches. Williams et al. (2003) describe the integration of cognitive behaviour therapy and cognitive rehabilitation for reducing symptoms and improving psychological outcome in two survivors of traumatic brain injury. They report on two patients admitted to a neuropsychological rehabilitation centre. One young man had sustained a closed head injury in a road traffic accident and one young woman had sustained a penetrating head injury during a knife attack. Both followed a goal-setting programme as described elsewhere in this book. Some goals were to address cognitive deficits, some were to address psychosocial roles, and some were to address symptoms of PTSD. CBT was used to manage the PTSD symptoms. This included use of a stress inoculation and graduated exposure to situations that were being avoided. Both these people reported significant improvements in their mood state and psychosocial roles.

BEHAVIOURAL MANAGEMENT OF LACK OF INSIGHT AND DENIAL OF DISABILITY

The importance of insight in successful engagement in rehabilitation has been widely discussed. Engaging patients in therapy activities when they do not have insight into their deficits or do not see the point of the therapy activities is one of the major challenges in brain-injury rehabilitation. Insight may develop over a period of time and is not a unitary phenomenon, in that different problem areas may be acknowledged at different times. The terminology can be confusing, as lack of awareness is sometimes used synonymously with lack of insight. While anosognosia or unawareness of deficit is believed to have a neurological basis, other factors such as emotionally based denial (Weinstein & Kahn, 1950), and disrupted cognitive functioning as the cause of unawareness of deficit (McGlynn & Schacter, 1989) have also been considered. Whilst insight is frequently assumed to be necessary to motivate rehabilitation efforts (Prigatano et al., 1986), high levels of insight at certain stages of recovery have also been noted as associated with depression and amotivational states (Powell, 1986). Herbert and Powell (1989) studied a broad group of disabled adults attending an employment rehabilitation programme and found that those who overestimated their potential for progress, i.e., were optimistic, made more progress than those who were underconfident, which suggested that under some circumstances inaccurate insight can be good if it is optimistic. One of the key issues in rehabilitation concerns the conditions under which insight should be actively promoted.

Crosson et al. (1989) conceptualised awareness deficits in terms of the patient's ability to be aware in different time-frames. Langer and Padrone (1992) described a model of insight based on the potential components of "not knowing", which include lack of information, inability to integrate the information, and inability to make appropriate inferences with that information. This can provide a useful framework to determine an appropriate intervention to raise insight and assist in engaging the patient with the rehabilitation programme. For example, an agitated or confused patient may need repeated presentation of basic information about their injury and their current placement, and reassurance that the staff are there to assist. This is often more usefully presented as a script read out by staff during some routine intervention, rather than as a question and answer orientation session which can elicit a series of erroneous responses that may serve to add to the confusion.

The inability to integrate the information successfully may mean that the person states that they have a problem in a particular area, but does not use that information to change their behaviour or coping strategies. Where the patient acknowledges in some settings that they have specific difficulties, for example, memory problems, but is resistant to suggestions to address this in any practical sense, it can be useful to involve them in group activities where the patients are set a task that relies on each one of them remembering and contributing. Peer pressure as well as peer modelling can have very positive influences. For example, one young man refused to use any sort of memory aid until he saw someone in a pub using a filofax. Behavioural recording by the therapist as well as by the patient can illustrate problems and be used to demonstrate successful strategies, provided the patient does not see direct confrontation as problematic.

Development of insight into deficits can be worked with over a longer period of time, although care must be taken to avoid confronting vulnerable patients with repeated failures. Pushing a patient prematurely to "know" what he or she cannot tolerate emotionally, by repeating or reinforcing the problem, may in itself be destructive (Levine & Zigler, 1975). Direct challenge or confrontation requires a strong therapeutic alliance between the patient and therapist if the patient is not to feel victimised by the process.

There are unfortunately cases where the combination of cognitive deficits and lack of insight limits the individual's ability to progress in rehabilitation. For example, Richard, aged 18, who had sustained a very severe head injury in a road traffic accident 2 years previously had great difficulty in remaining focused on the small steps needed to achieve his goal of walking. He had been treated at an inpatient rehabilitation facility for a year, where he made limited physical progress, remaining wheelchair dependent, and with bilateral memory impairment and cognitive problems with poor reasoning skills and poor impulse control. His family wished to care for him at home and he was rehoused in a

TABLE 7.1
Treatment session contract agreed with Richard aimed at controlling the time
spent in discussion during each treatment session

THERAPY PROGRAMME

SHORT TERM AIMS:

1. **Sitting to standing**
   Richard is able to get from sitting position to standing using the correct procedure as
   written down by his physiotherapist. He should maintain his standing balance for a
   period of 5 minutes.

   Richard agrees to do this 3 times per session by 14th February

2. **Standing to sitting**
   Richard is able to get from standing to sitting position again using the correct procedure, as
   written down by his physiotherapist.

   Richard agrees to do this 3 times per session by 14th February

SIGNED: SIGNED:

WITNESSED BY:

---

wheelchair-accessible flat. He attended a multidisciplinary outpatient rehabilitation service, initially three times per week. His main goal was to walk. Although
the physiotherapist felt that he had the physical skills to progress at least to
walking short distances, and structured his programme into small achievable
stages, Richard was unable to make the link between these stages and his ultim-
ate goal of walking. Richard was also unable to see the contribution of other
activities, for example, his occupational therapy programme, towards his main
goal. In each session, therapy time was being used repeatedly to explain the
rationale for treatment rather than carrying out the agreed treatment programme.
Eventually a set of written contracts were drawn up which specified the exact
treatment goals within a session, and the date at which this would be reviewed
as part of his longer-term goal planning. An example of one of the treatment
session contracts is shown in Table 7.1.

It was intended to use these contracts initially only in treatment sessions, and
if the idea proved successful then it would be extended to other situations including the home environment. Unfortunately, even with the written information and
recording of achievement, Richard proved to be unable to comply consistently
with these tasks. His memory and reasoning skills were such that he remained

convinced that he had carried out each stage with "110% effort" within each session, even when this was clearly not the case. He and his family lost confidence in the staff as he failed to progress and after further discussion he moved on to attend a further education college course for people with special needs, still unable to walk but expressing his determination to do so.

BEHAVIOURAL MANAGEMENT OF APATHY AND POOR MOTIVATION

People with a brain injury are often described as having a problem with motivation. Some patients will report it themselves, usually with a phrase such as "I seem to have lost my 'get up and go'" or "I want to do things but just don't seem to get round to them". In many cases it is the professionals who describe the person with the brain injury as "poorly motivated" or "non-compliant with treatment" or a family member who may say that the person has become "lazy" or "doesn't want to do anything".

In addition to the problems created by cognitive deficits, lack of insight, and mood disorders, other explanations for reduced motivation include fatigue, lack of drive, and lack of initiation. Reduction of drive shows in general lethargy, as well as in problems of motivation. Patients with problems of initiation may have goals they wish to achieve but have difficulty generating or activating the appropriate goal-directed behaviour.

In the active rehabilitation phase staff and family members should be encouraged to arouse the apathetic patient and encourage them into activities. The high incidence of agitated patients on brain-injury units means that it is these more voluble and more active patients who occupy staff time and attention. This can exacerbate one of the problems in rehabilitating patients with reduced levels of drive or poor initiation, in that they produce fewer behaviours in general, and are therefore less likely to benefit from reinforcers. This can mean that they are sometimes more difficult to work with than are agitated patients. The lack of drive or the raised level of fatigue means that invitations or requests to engage in therapy or participate in social activities may be refused because they are perceived to require too much effort. Some patients are happy to agree to do things but then fail to initiate the response, and "just don't get round to it". As a result patients can spend much of their time sitting or lying around, and they have to be encouraged to attend therapy, take care of personal hygiene, and in some instances to eat.

Where lack of initiation limits participation, a system of regular prompts can be helpful to "kick-start" an activity. This may take the form of verbal or physical prompts by staff or family members, but it can be made more acceptable to some patients if an external device such as an alarm clock, a beeping watch, or some form of pager system provides the prompts. Activities can be linked together so that the need for repeated prompting can be reduced, a common example being the chaining together of the morning washing and dressing routine. Where problems with apraxia and with sequencing actions are contributing to the difficulties with washing and dressing routines, repeated practice, written checklists, and fading of both written and verbal prompts can help patients regain their independence, and form a routine part of many rehabilitation packages.

Some patients who are clearly capable of washing and dressing independently or with minimal assistance may refuse to do so. Further analysis usually identifies some disturbance of mood or emotion as a key factor here. Frustration at lack of personal progress or delays in placement can result in previously capable patients seeming to lose skills. Interventions to address these underlying or specific difficulties may take time to be effective, but for reasons of hygiene a more immediate intervention may be necessary. Rather than enter into confrontative or prescriptive statements, it is often more successful to use appropriate forced choices, for example, "Will you have your bath first or your shave?". Another option is positive enticement for example, "I've run your bath to the temperature you like it, it's all ready for you now" (see Rothwell, LaVigna, & Willis, 1999, for further examples of this approach).

Behavioural contracts can be effective, for example, an agreement with a patient to bathe each evening in exchange for a cinema trip at the weekend. As with all such contracts, the rewards need to be relevant to the individual and deliverable by the staff. Maintaining motivation over a prolonged period can be difficult, and staff, family, and the individual themselves will need to renegotiate contracts and rewards to adapt to changing situations.

BEHAVIOURAL MANAGEMENT OF NON-ATTENDANCE AND NON-COOPERATION WITH REHABILITATION

In the early phase of recovery non-cooperation with treatment can be life-threatening, for example, where a patient's agitated behaviour is such that it prevents appropriate nursing and medical care such as cleaning a wound or changing a gastrostomy tube. While it is possible to use sedative medication, particularly in an emergency, this is not always appropriate as it interferes with other components of the rehabilitation programme, and is not a long-term solution. Although in general the role of behavioural management in the early stages post-injury where the patient is likely to be in post traumatic amnesia is limited, environmental manipulations to reduce confusions, such as putting personal possessions or photographs by the bedside, can be helpful. Howard (1988) for example describes the use of environmental restructuring as well as response-contingent reinforcers to facilitate managing a patient with impaired alertness, attention and memory deficits, rapid fatigue, confusion, and disorientation. The main danger is the threat to the physical welfare of the patient, although at times the safety of other patients or staff may be at risk. The appropriate use of restraints or medication is described in more detail by Eames et al. (1990).

The general advice for staff and relatives is to use structure, consistency, and repetition to prevent or minimise agitated outbursts. Yuen and Benzing (1996) describe a range of "redirection" approaches that are particularly useful for managing prolonged periods of confusion and agitation. They list six techniques to redirect a confused individual to engage in a desired activity, and provide case illustrations. These include supportive guidance by presenting requests without giving the choice of "no" as a response, but not rushing or confronting the client; cognitive set change through pre-orientation, e.g., talking to a client about eating and food 5–10 minutes before lunch to enhance compliance with the cue to go to the dining room to eat; focus shift to increase compliance, e.g., the client claimed to have taken a shower, and rather than confront this directly, the therapist helped them check whether their hair was wet and then prompted them to wash this; appropriate use of humour; cognitive re-enactment of premorbid behaviour by linking the current request to a previous established pattern of behaviour; direct attention through reward and rationale, e.g., emphasising the benefits to the individual of carrying out the activity requested rather than not doing so. Yuen and Benzing also list five approaches to redirect an individual from a source of confusion and agitation in order to prevent or reduce further behavioural outbursts. These include refocusing with a rationale, which is useful for clients demonstrating catastrophic reactions to less familiar situations, for example where the client does not recognise the environment and becomes agitated because they think they do not live there. It involves accepting the client's confusion by non-confrontation and guiding the client to refocus on a related issue such as the familiarity of the accompanying therapist. Other examples include channelling inappropriate behaviour, physical exercise, redirection through meaningful or attention-getting distraction, and intermittent ignoring with re-intervention. The authors acknowledge that the classification is arbitrary and that the techniques one uses will fall into more than one category, but the paper does provide clear illustrations of the rationale for applying each technique.

In one of the few reports of behavioural management approaches in the acute illness phase Slifer, Cataldo, and Kurtz (1995) described the use of operant conditioning-based procedures with an 8-year-old girl recovering from brain trauma and subsequent neurosurgery. The child was still in post traumatic amnesia at 77 days post-initial brain trauma, when the programme began, and did not become significantly more oriented for a further 38 days. The programme treated screaming, non-cooperation, and aggression with differential positive reinforcement techniques. Behavioural treatment during sessions consisted of adult attention and verbal praise contingent on cooperation without disruptive behaviour. Stickers or a ribbon were provided by the therapists and paired with positive social reinforcement. If a disruptive behaviour occurred, the therapist verbally prompted the child to use words (e.g., "it hurts") as an appropriate alternative behaviour. If, after two such prompts, disruptive behaviour occurred again, the therapist withheld the token or removed the ribbon, and the session temporarily continued using gentle physical guidance, if necessary, without social attention or praise. After 1 minute of calm, cooperative behaviour, the ribbon was re-presented, or a sticker awarded and social reinforcement contingencies resumed. A preselected tangible reinforcer (snack, prize, preferred activity) was provided if the child cooperated during the session with no more than two occurrences of disruptive behaviour. During the last 2 weeks of the inpatient programme the tangible reinforcers were gradually faded by reducing their frequency across the day until only social reinforcers were required.

Behavioural interventions can also be effective with very impaired patients or with patients where difficulties in the early phase of rehabilitation have resulted in ongoing non-cooperation. Alderman, Shepherd, and Youngson (1992) describe an intervention with a young man with potential for greater physical independence but who regularly had outbursts when asked to work on standing tolerance and posture within physiotherapy sessions. The behavioural analysis identified a combination of raised anxiety and poor tolerance of frustration as the underlying factors, and the behaviour itself resulted in him successfully avoiding greater anxiety or frustration. The programme initially rewarded him for achieving small steps in his physical progress, and this progress became in itself sufficiently rewarding for the patient that the reward system could be withdrawn without adverse effect. Other studies too have demonstrated the benefits of behavioural management in increasing participation within sessions and treatment activities (Hegel, 1988; Tate, 1987). Meyerson, Kerr, and Michael (1967) showed that participation within sessions could be encouraged by social praise. Informal observation of a patient's attention to a typing task indicated that the therapist had been differentially responding to off-task behaviour by paying attention to the patient primarily when he stopped working to call for help, ask a question, or complain. The work was moved to a less distracting area, social attention was contingent on a gradually increasing criterion of work completed, and ignoring off-task demands.

During the rehabilitation phase non-cooperation often takes the form of failure to attend sessions. Where this is based on underlying problems with cognition and memory, a behavioural approach that circumvents the cognitive deficit rather than relying on the disrupted memory and learning skills can be very successful. Zencius et al. (1989) described two cases of non-attendance which on investigation were found to be a result of the patients not remembering what was expected of them. In one case the client left the vocational training site without permission, taking unauthorised breaks. Reinforcers such as coffee or money had been tried in an effort to promote regular attendance. A contract that outlined a move to a new residence also failed to decrease the behaviour. The antecedent control technique of placing a poster with the appropriate break times was tried and greatly reduced the frequency of unauthorised breaks. In a second case, the client was not attending therapy sessions. A consequent management technique was tried—paying the client for attending sessions—but it was discontinued because it was ineffective. A written invitation to attend presented 5 minutes prior to each session, explaining what the session was, who the therapist was, and a map showing the way to class, resulted in nearly 100% attendance.

Within a community or outpatient setting, where there are fewer opportunities to control the reinforcers for specific behaviours, behavioural contracts are often the treatment of choice for managing cooperation with treatment. Their effectiveness depends on the degree of co-existing cognitive problems, the level of impulsivity displayed by the person with the brain injury when the more structured environment is removed, and by the extent to which the extended family and social network is engaged in a consistent approach. Some of these difficulties were highlighted earlier in this chapter in the discussion about engaging Richard in active rehabilitation through the use of behavioural contracts within sessions. A more effective use of contracts to maintain cooperation within a community setting is described in the next case example. In this example, the person with a brain injury had information about his deficits, he could understand the effects of his actions, but was unable to prevent himself acting impulsively and thereby undermining his own progress.

Kevin had sustained a severe head injury in a road traffic accident when he was 16. He was discharged home to the care of his parents at 2 months post-injury and although he subsequently received outpatient physiotherapy treatment he did not have access to any other rehabilitation. Just prior to the accident he had left school and obtained his first job in a warehouse. He was finally referred for rehabilitation 9 years post-injury, at which time he was living in a one-bedroom flat close to his parents who continued to provide daily support to him, although he tended to minimise their role in maintaining his independence.

Since his injury Kevin had tried a number of jobs and training schemes which had "never lasted long". He spent his time watching TV, going to the pub, and playing fruit machines. He had had two girlfriends since the accident, but neither of these had developed into serious relationships.

Multidisciplinary team assessment identified that Kevin had significant attentional deficits, affecting his acquisition of information, and rendering him highly susceptible to distraction. He had some slight problems with movement affecting his ability to balance. He was independent in his personal care, but was not independent in his ability to manage his budget or care for his home. His main deficit though was his unrealistic and inappropriate goal setting and his poor impulse control. When the results were fed back to Kevin he disagreed with the description of his ability to care for himself, claiming that he did manage his budget accurately and that his family did not need to provide significant levels of support. The agreed initial aims of the programme therefore were to assess further the level of home care support required and, as an enticement

TABLE 7.2
Kevin: Programme agreed to achieve independence in cleaning his flat

Targets	Date set	Date reviewed
Kevin to clean flat windows on inside once per fortnight	12th April	Reviewed 28th April. Goal achieved
As above—PLUS Kevin will clean the bathroom—bath, washbasin, and toilet	28th April	Reviewed 11th May. Goal achieved
Clean windows on inside/outside once per fortnight Clean bathroom 1 × per week Hoover/tidy 3 × per week	11th May	Reviewed 21st May. Goal partially achieved
As above Record ALL cleaning tasks	21st May	Reviewed 4th June. Goal achieved

for Kevin, to explore opportunities to retrain for employment, as this was his stated goal.

Kevin was very persuasive verbally and could talk his way into a job or convince a therapist that he had completed a task as agreed. It was essential therefore to have a tight system of contracts and written agreements with him. For example, it rapidly became evident that in spite of his protestations about independence within his home, Kevin was not keeping his flat clean and that his parents continued to provide significant levels of input. With an agreed withdrawal of support from his parents, a programme of independence in cleaning was established (see Table 7.2).

It took time to establish regular recording of activities and establish the pattern of contracts. After approximately 6 months this was achieved and Kevin was encouraged to attempt a limited amount of voluntary work. Up until that time some progress had been made in his home management skills, particularly in relation to his laundry and his cleaning routines. Unfortunately, Kevin found the voluntary work more stimulating, seeing this as a route to employment and he was unable to restrain himself from taking on extra hours of voluntary work. As a result, cooperation with the cleaning and home maintenance programmed ceased. Another set of contracts was therefore instituted to control the number of hours of voluntary work that he was allowed to take on.

The other major problem continued to be Kevin's poor budgeting skills, where the initial targets had not been achieved. After a break the programme was restarted but it still proved difficult for Kevin to achieve the identified targets (see Table 7.3).

Three months on, Kevin had succeeded in controlling the amount of voluntary work he took on, and had re-established his laundry and cleaning programme.

TABLE 7.3
Kevin: Programme to achieve independence in budgeting

Targets	Date set	Date reviewed
1. Give half of Giro money to mother 2. Record all expenditure	12th April	Reviewed 28th April. Goal partially achieved
1 & 2 as above—PLUS 3. Kevin to give his Dad £9 per week	28th April	Reviewed 11th May. Goal partially achieved
Programme temporarily suspended		
Record all expenditure for week	6th September	Reviewed 20th September. Goal not achieved
Record all expenditure for week	20th September	Reviewed 3rd October. Goal not achieved
Record all expenditure for week	3rd October	Reviewed 17th October. Goal not achieved

However, he could not control his expenditure and this was causing considerable strain in his relationship with his parents, since it was usually to them that he went to borrow more money. A further contract was then drawn up in the presence of his parents, occupational therapist, and social worker (see Table 7.4).

In addition to the voluntary work Kevin was now attending a local mental health daycentre three times a week. As with every new activity, Kevin tended to become very enthusiastic, and to lose track of the other parts of the programme that were already established. Yet another contract was required, this time spelling out the exact times that he could attend the centre and the purpose of each visit, for example, for the "Men's Group" on Friday mornings. Kevin needed to be reminded that the centre was "not a drop in centre for tea and biscuits" and that his timetable there was to be negotiated in advance with his key worker.

With the pattern of intervention and the level of continuing support required more clearly identified, it became possible for the rehabilitation team to gradually withdraw their direct interventions and hand over the package of support to the local services. It took a prolonged period of time for the local services to recognise the requirement to keep Kevin to his contracts and to prepare new ones as situations occurred. If there was a loophole Kevin would find it, so in that sense he continued to fail to comply with the contracts, but he did go along with them up to the point where they could be effective in maintaining considerable control over his activities. It was also fortunate that his mistakes were frequent enough and obvious enough to be identified and resolved fairly rapidly, provided the situation was monitored regularly.

TABLE 7.4
Kevin: Contract drawn up to address continuing problems with budgeting

Contract in relation to budgeting

Persons present: **Kevin, father, mother, social worker, OT**
Date:

It was agreed that Kevin's current system for budgeting his money was not being adhered to and that he was regularly harassing his mother for more. This was discussed and the following agreements made:

(1) Kevin will receive £5.00 from one of his parents on a Monday, Wednesday, Friday, and Saturday.
(2) It is **Kevin's responsibility** to make this money last from each payment to the next and to prove that he is capable of budgeting successfully.
(3) If Kevin's money runs out he will **not** harass his mother for more. Should he ask or even hint at his mother for more money she is to ring either the social worker or the OT immediately.
(4) Kevin will **not** borrow money from any other persons or source but will either do without, or ask his father. His father is entitled to use his discretion and distribute extra money as he feels necessary.

Signed:

Father	**Mother**	**Kevin**	**Social Worker**	**OT**

His family members were actively involved in the negotiations from an early stage, and although at times it was difficult for them to maintain consistency, they understood the rationale for the approach and could see the benefits.

Within a community setting, contracts can never be absolutely watertight, as there are too many variables and potential pitfalls. With adequate supervision to identify and solve problems as they emerge, a system of contracts can be used to maintain a greater level of independence in spite of significant cognitive deficits and poor impulse control that would otherwise prevent cooperation with a more loosely structured regime.

VULNERABLE ADULTS AND CONSENT TO TREATMENT

It has already been asserted in this chapter that reduced insight is one of the greatest challenges in brain-injury rehabilitation. A particularly difficult area to address is the impact of reduced insight on the ability of the individual to give consent to the treatment. In the early stages post-injury an injured person may not be capable of consenting to treatment, and non-cooperation is likely to be the result of confusion and agitation. Although these problems usually resolve over time, one unfortunate consequence is that some patients can be discharged early from hospitals if they insist that they are recovered, and without appropriate support these patients are easily lost to follow-up services and can find themselves excluded from or failing to access treatment or help that they need or could benefit from.

Once the acute phase of confusion and agitation has passed, the injured individual may still lack insight but is usually assumed to be capable in a legal sense. The law makes a presumption of capacity until proven otherwise, and this is not usually addressed unless conflicts arise or there is a specific legal reason to challenge the assumption of capacity. Most rehabilitation programmes seek to inform, encourage, and persuade individuals of the benefits of the treatment approach. The use of behavioural contracts, for example, is dependent on the patient's willingness to comply with rehabilitation even though they are cognitively unable to put this into practice without the structure of the contracting process. Successful programmes are usually those where there is agreement from the patient and their family that this is an appropriate and helpful way forward. In many cases the patient may agree even though their capacity to fully comprehend their deficits and their needs is questionable.

Whether it is as a result of cognitive problems or lack of insight, the consequences of failing to comply with certain ongoing medical treatment such as anticonvulsant medication, or with safety precautions such as contraceptive advice, can potentially be extremely serious. However, where the patient is an adult and the situation does not constitute a medical emergency, there are no powers to enforce treatment. This can create problems for vulnerable adults such as Sally whose cooperation with treatment was highly variable. Sally was an 18-year-old female injured 2 years previously in a road traffic accident, from which she made an excellent physical recovery but which left her with severe cognitive impairment including severe memory impairment and limited reasoning skills. She also developed post traumatic epilepsy for which long-term treatment with anticonvulsant medication was required. With no stable family background Sally was placed in a succession of local authority placements, some of which were able to keep track of her behaviour, but all of which ultimately broke down as she disappeared for days at a time, returning with bruises on her body and no clear account of where she had been. Her inability to remember from day to day meant that she was unable to consistently comply with any community-based programme, including taking her medication regularly. As a consequence of her behaviour she was also at risk of unplanned pregnancy, but could not reliably take contraceptive precautions. Her suggestibility made her vulnerable. She would be compliant with suggestions from professionals involved which could allow her GP to provide long-term contraceptive protection, but she was equally compliant with suggestions from others such that she would disappear again and not be accessible to the professionals involved. Cooperation with ongoing recommended medical treatment could not therefore be guaranteed.

Vulnerability can also take the form of exploitation by others, and unfortunately the brain-injured person may be sufficiently capable to refuse to take precautions or listen to advice, but not able to prevent financial and sometimes criminal exploitation. For example, Shane sustained a severe head injury in an RTA at the age of 18. He suffered frontal contusions, and in the early phase post-injury was agitated and aggressive. He made a rapid physical recovery without insight into other deficits and became angry about staying in the rehabilitation unit. His family was keen to have him at home and early discharge was agreed, although the staff had reservations. His family attempted to contain his behaviour over the next 2 years, as he continued to reject direct intervention. Following the death of his mother, the family acknowledged that he was uncontrollable and he was admitted to a rehabilitation unit. At this stage he was displaying impulsive behaviour, poor money management, and some episodes of aggression, which were linked to the consumption of drugs and alcohol. He was difficult to contain within the unit, as he had had his driving licence returned and if confronted with problems would take off in his car. Following a period of several months at the rehabilitation facility, Shane was gradually re-integrated into a form of supervised independence in his local community. Shane continued to reject close supervision and would not agree to a structured programme of activities. He proved to be vulnerable to exploitation by others who used him as a fall guy for various petty crimes. Shane was unable to see this as a problem, and for many months could not be persuaded by family or professionals to comply with treatment recommendations that might have protected him. Eventually the situation was stabilised, by repeated efforts from family and professionals and the recruitment of a new team of support workers who were able to form a good relationship with Shane.

In the absence of a clear framework for interventions with patients with limited ability to make informed consent or decisions about their lifestyle and the effect this has on others, clinicians work on the principle of the best interest of the individual patient. At times this can result in difficult decisions. Avoiding paternalistic decisions, allowing people to take risks, but recognising that these are not necessarily informed decisions, form part of the challenge of providing a long-term support service to people with acquired brain injury. Such decisions are becoming increasingly relevant as more people are moving into community-based care packages. Support workers and care managers are faced on a daily basis with questions of risk management and personal liberty. For example, if individuals want to spend their money on cheap jewellery at the expense of the week's food budget, how is this negotiated? If an individual wants to spend the afternoon watching pornographic videos, how does the support worker respond? If a person with brain injury rejects the support package, at what point does the individual become so unsafe or so vulnerable that the system does intervene? While the concept of "best interests of the patient" can be helpful in these cases, this is an area where clinicians would welcome a more helpful legal framework that specifically addressed the issues relating to acquired brain injury.

SUMMARY

Non-cooperation with treatment following brain injury can be the result of the deficits that either prevent the individual recognising or understanding the problem, or prevent them implementing strategies to overcome the identified problem. Mood disorders often form part of a complex mixture of factors influencing motivation and cooperation. Behavioural management approaches can be used successfully both with severe and more moderately impaired individuals to allow progress to be made. However the questions of what constitutes "informed consent" and what happens to vulnerable adults when they exercise their right to refuse treatment or support have not yet been adequately addressed.

CHAPTER 8

Educating staff and family members in the long-term management of behaviour disorders

STAFF SUPPORT AND TRAINING

Support for staff

Working with patients who have sustained a brain injury is stressful and psycho-logically demanding. At times there are threats or actual episodes of physical assault. Staff members are vulnerable to a number of problems that interfere with effective treatment of patients including "burnout", anger at patients and their families, and fighting for power and control. These problems are not unique to brain injury and can arise in a range of residential settings. However, there are a number of factors within the field of brain-injury rehabilitation that render staff particularly susceptible to stress (Greif & Matarazzo, 1982; Sargent, 1989).

The work often includes seeing another person's distress. The frustration and helplessness of the patient can be mirrored by the staff member who feels powerless to significantly alter the patient's condition. This can be particularly problematic where the staff member identifies with the patient, through similar age or interests, or in longer-term care facilities where the staff member may have a long-term involvement with the patient. For many staff there is usually at least one moment or one patient who reminds them of their own vulnerability; that something similar could happen to them or to someone they care about.

The implementation of management approaches, for example the withdrawal of a reinforcer, may initially produce a strong response from the patient, either anger or distress, which can be stressful for the staff to observe even when they recognise the treatment rationale and know the safeguards that are in place to protect the patient.

For some staff, recognition of the limited resources and options available to particular patients can be an additional source of stress. Staff may become "advocates" for an individual where they feel that a proposed placement is less than desirable, or where they observe discrimination or intolerance in the workplace, community, or in service provision.

People with brain injuries do not say thank you very often. They are usually struggling to deal with so many problems themselves that they appear self-centred and rarely appreciate the role of the staff surrounding them. New or inexperienced care staff often find this particularly stressful and may try to impose their values or views of acceptable behaviour. Even experienced staff who recognise that they should not expect approval or appreciation from patients can find it difficult when there is little positive feedback. The shock and warm glow that accompanies the few occasions when gratitude or thanks is expressed is an indication of how rarely this occurs.

The slow progress made in rehabilitation by some patients provides little reinforcement for staff about the success or efficacy of their interventions. This can result in the care staff doubting their competence, which in turn can exaggerate feelings of helplessness or low self-esteem.

Staff may be the recipients of the strong emotions felt by relatives. Anger can be directed at staff because they are there, but cannot do what the relative wants them to do, i.e., make the injured person well again. Staff are also not perfect, and they do make mistakes or fail to communicate, which families find difficult to accept. Unless such issues are addressed the team may become split, as different staff members approach the family in different ways, or the team may as a whole become alienated from the family or blame the family for limited progress (Carberry, 1990; Stern, Sazbon, Becker & Costeff, 1988).

If family breakdown occurs as a result of the strains imposed by the brain injury, the staff involved have to be careful not to become drawn into what will inevitably be a highly charged emotional situation. Issues such as confidentiality have to considered carefully if the patient does not wish information to be shared with some family members. Support for different family members may be affected and staff can have multiple perspectives both on the causes of the problems and on the ways forward for the individuals concerned (Webster, Daisley, & King, 1999).

Strategies to support staff

The key area is education and training. Staff who understand the nature of the disability, the course of treatment, and future options can place the treatment programme and the individuals within it in an appropriate context. Education too about the effect of brain injury on the extended family can help to reduce conflicts between staff and relatives.

Good communications are necessary within the treating team to ensure that all voices are heard. Staff who are listened to and who see the effect of their actions are better able to deal with a broad range of stressful situations.

Clear and reasonable expectations of change should be communicated with staff. Improvements can be charted and feedback provided to staff.

Staff should be encouraged to work with a range of patients within the unit to provide a more varied schedule.

Staff should be encouraged to take their planned breaks within the working day, and to make use of annual leave entitlements and other time off.

Staff support groups, informal and formal supervision, and good colleague relationships should be encouraged. Team days and outings that are informal and social can help staff to feel part of a group that is mutually supportive.

Staff should be encouraged to have a life outside work to ensure that they retain a sense of perspective.

Staff training

All staff working with people with brain injuries need training in whatever setting they are working. The specifics of the training will differ depending on whether it is an acute or sub-acute ward, residential rehabilitation unit, or an outpatient or community service. There are however three core areas that need to be addressed.

Training in specific disorders and challenging behaviours

Staff need training to prepare them to deal with common problems associated with brain injury. Once the need for acute medical management has passed, many people with brain injuries are treated or placed within settings where there is a high proportion of non-medical and non-nursing trained staff involved with the patient on a daily basis. Such staff are likely to need training on seizure disorders, diabetes management, and dysphagia as well as recognition of the importance of other changes in behaviour, for example, in sleep or appetite patterns, or withdrawal from social contacts which might indicate a mood disorder. Staff need to know what to report and to whom. It is often helpful to have a checklist or suggested headings to assist in appropriate record keeping.

Staff also need training in the management of agitation and aggression. Factors that escalate situations can include staff attitudes and assumptions as well as a range of environmental constraints. There is therefore a need for all staff, but particularly the direct care workers, to receive training in how to diffuse situations and to avoid harm. It is essential to ensure that staff, particularly unqualified staff, are taught about the organic underpinnings of many of these behaviours. Without this knowledge there is a tendency to blame the individual or to attribute to them a greater degree of control over their behaviour than they actually have. It can be helpful to train the staff in the basic principles of behavioural recording so that they can learn to observe the antecedents of agitation and aggression, and to identify what can be changed by them, by the client, or by family members. It is also useful to provide guidance on environmental safety considerations, such as office design, unbreakable glass etc., as well as policies on home visits, including informing colleagues of the visit and having an arrangement for checking-in following completion of the visit. In more recent years the enormous increase in community provision has highlighted the issue of personal safety, but the need to prevent assaults on professional carers was recognised many years ago, for example see Davies (1989). Many aggressive situations within community settings can be prevented by appropriate management—however, there are exceptions and staff need to know the specific policies and procedures to follow in the event of a situation escalating. In some settings staff may need to be trained in appropriate use of restraint, but this should always be considered as a final step and should only be carried out by trained staff.

In outpatient and community settings the emphasis is predominantly on the use of diffusion techniques and awareness of environmental safety. This includes training on the appropriate layout of treatment areas and waiting areas to reduce agitation and aggression, as well as considerations of safety on community and home visits.

For staff employed to provide a care package within a patient's home, questions may arise concerning the limits of their ability to control the actions of their patient, and consideration should be given to appropriate supervision and support for workers faced with conflicting demands within such settings. Training should be provided concerning the risks and responsibilities of working with vulnerable adults.

Knowledge of brain injury: Its causes, effects, and implications for behaviour

Staff need to understand the initial impact of and sequence of events following a brain injury and specifically they need to understand the organic underpinnings of behaviour. They need to be familiar with basic neuroanatomy, in particular the major areas of the brain and their functions. Many staff will have been trained or have worked within psychiatric or social support settings where there is an emphasis on self-empowerment and encouraging individuals to take responsibility for their symptoms and their recovery. Given the organic nature of the symptoms of a brain-injured person it is often difficult for the individual to make choices, however highly motivated, and the role of the staff is necessarily different.

Staff also need to be familiar with the care pathway that people with brain injuries experience so that they can recognise the relevance of their particular place in the process. They need to know what the patients will be doing in their setting and the type of outcomes that can realistically be expected.

In long-term care or community settings there is a particular need to train staff in the organic underpinnings of behaviour. Many misunderstandings and misattributions occur where staff assume a level of control or insight that the person with a brain injury does not have, in spite of the appearance of their actions. The implications of this in terms of service provision are enormous. Many people with brain injury do not receive services because the assessment of their needs does not take into account their lack of insight. Skilled interviewers can elicit problems and requests for assistance that are missed by those who do not understand the nature of the condition.

Specific implementation of programme and therapy guidelines

The staff implementing behaviour programmes are not usually those who wrote them. It is helpful therefore to ensure that staff have initial training in the core principles of behaviour management (Foster, 1988; Peters, Gluck, & McCormick, 1992).

When a new programme is developed, there needs to be an identified person to be responsible for training all who will be implementing the programme. This may be one person or an identified pathway for transfer of the information. It is helpful if the written programmes follow an identifiable format. This assists staff to become familiar with what is required and encourages consistency. Within each programme there needs to be a brief rationale so that staff can identify not only what problem is being addressed but why. The target behaviour needs to be operationally defined, and examples recorded. The objective of the programme should be clearly stated so that staff can recognise that the goal is achieved. The procedure must be clear, concise, and broken into basic steps. Finally, there must be a clear statement of the information to be recorded and when and how this should be done. Recording sheets that follow a regular format will be completed more efficiently. However well motivated or trained, staff do not maintain programmes that are too complex.

Many staff underestimate their level of skill in observing and recording behaviour. Regular feedback and supervision can reinforce good practice and reduce the occurrence of poor or sloppy practice.

When patients transfer between facilities or approach discharge to the community there is always a risk that important behavioural management information will be lost. It is good practice for staff from the new placement to spend time with the individual and the existing staff (Foster, 1988). It can also be helpful to have access to a system of follow-up advice, at least for a short term, to troubleshoot problems that emerge before the new staff have gained the same level of familiarity with the individual and their needs.

FAMILY SUPPORT AND FAMILY TRAINING

The emotional toll on family members, from the initial crisis of life or death to the long-term burden of care in the community, has been extensively documented. The struggle to come to terms with the cognitive and personality changes in the brain-injured person, and the mourning for the loss of potential, is described throughout the literature (Brooks, Campsie, Symington, Beattie, & McKinlay, 1986; Kreutzer, Gervasio, & Camplair, 1994; Lezak, 1987; Livingston & Brooks, 1988; Oddy, Humphrey, & Uttley, 1978). Many people with brain injury show emotional and behavioural disorders, which in a proportion of cases are sufficiently severe to require intensive and specialist inpatient treatment, but which for the majority of cases affects the ability of the brain-injured person to interact appropriately within their family and community. This places an enormous burden on families, and the consequences for the injured person are seen in their increasing social isolation (Kozloff, 1987; Zencius & Wesolowski, 1999), low mood (Thomsen, 1984), and poor employment prospects (Possl, Jurgensmeyer, Karlbauer, Wenz, & Goldenberg, 2001; Sander et al., 1996). Nevertheless the potential for many brain-injury treatment programmes to address the long-term needs of their clients is affected by their limited ability to generalise unless they are able to engage the family in supporting the aims of the programme. This requires education and understanding on the part of the family, as well as a willingness to participate. Without the support of the family, many rehabilitation programmes are not able to succeed. Family support programmes have been offered from acute care through to long-term community support, and behaviour management principles have influenced both education programmes and more psychotherapeutically oriented support programmes for families of people with head injury.

Behavioural management and family support within rehabilitation settings

In acute rehabilitation settings the emphasis is usually on the patient's medical rather than behavioural problems. The family may be involved in a "heroic vigil" at the patient's bedside, with the major focus of their concern being the life or death scenario and subsequently the relief at their relative's survival. Within such a setting the approach is predominantly one of medical and nursing care and there is little scope for establishing the level of integration and consistency required by a behavioural approach.

When patients move on to the rehabilitation phase there is usually access to medical, nursing, and therapy staff, but few units in the United Kingdom are able to provide the level of structure and support that can cope with difficult behaviour as a matter of routine. Most brain-injury rehabilitation is carried out on orthopaedic and medical wards or in more generic sub-acute rehabilitation units in which the ethos often remains that of a more traditional "care" approach, where therapy time and the ward routine do not fill the waking day, and there are extended periods of unstructured time that families come to fill. In most rehabilitation units the emphasis of family intervention programmes at this stage tends to be about support for their grief, acknowledgement of their distress, and provision of general information about brain injury, rather than more overt advice about behavioural management or treatment guidelines. For example, in the management of patients still in post traumatic amnesia or in confusional states, staff may be attempting to orientate the patient rather than test their memory, to be consistent in the information that they provide, and to stick to a routine of activities as far as is practical. Family members, who are often present for significant periods of time or planning to have the patient home on weekend leave are usually advised only on an ad hoc basis about how to approach their relative and are rarely shown an appropriate model of interaction, given written guidelines, or reinforced for "good practice".

Family members can therefore receive mixed messages about their role and little direct advice about how to adapt their approach both in the short and long term. There are some examples of good practice that encourage families to provide general stimulation in the form of a range of specific tasks that encourage the client to think and react to the environment (Novack, Bergquist, & Bennett, 1992). While Novack did not claim that such generalised stimulation would in itself necessarily benefit the client directly, he argued that it focused the attention and energy of family members and helped them to distinguish between organised stimulation and passive activities, such as watching television. Unfortunately this approach is relatively rare and it is more common for families to accept and learn the approaches to managing physical care but to remain confused about how to handle cognitive and psychosocial sequelae.

While the emotional needs of family members and the desire for information are well established, the efficacy and function of programmes that have attempted to address these needs at an early stage are less clear. It has been argued that education is particularly useful at the early stages of recovery when there are uncertainties and unanswered questions (Rosenthal & Muir, 1983), and clinical experience recognises that family members do ask repeatedly for information. However, other studies have reported that even when families have had access to an education programme at an early stage, they remain dissatisfied when interviewed later with the amount and type of information they received about the nature and extent of injury (Jacobs, 1991). Acknowledgement of the distress felt within families has been addressed by psychotherapeutic interventions as well as by advice and education. At the sub-acute stage psychotherapeutic interventions with family members, either group or individual, are limited in their effectiveness by unrealistic expectations for patient recovery, denial of deficits, and emotional shock, although it can be argued that family group work at this stage can lay foundations for subsequent interventions (Jackson & Gouvier, 1992).

It is probable that for many families the process of adjustment affects their ability to take in information. Education programmes at an early stage, therefore, while responding to an expressed need, are not sufficient in themselves to address that need. However, they may, like the family group work, serve an important function in establishing communication between the clinicians and the family. Nevertheless a more overt or explicit behavioural programme of feedback and involvement of family members would be an important step in preparing families for the situation post-discharge.

Outpatient and community rehabilitation

It is at the point of discharge into the home environment that the requirement for consistency and structure becomes more apparent. Families as well as the injured person have to "learn" new skills and how to apply these skills to what may be a very different life situation from that pre-injury (Diehl, 1983). Although the need for a consistent approach by staff and family was present from the acute phase onwards, family members may not recognise the importance of this, in spite of family education programmes, until the patient has extended periods of home leave or is discharged. Families are generally ill-equipped or reluctant to impose a highly structured environment when the patient arrives home (Sbordone, 1988). As a result of their poor understanding of brain injury, and often as a consequence of their own period of denial, their demands frequently exceed the patient's ability to encode and process information, which results in considerable cognitive and communicative confusion and emotional outbursts that the family often fails to comprehend or accept. It becomes difficult to structure the patient's environment at home in order to facilitate the recovery of impaired attention and information-processing capacities.

The challenges to successful implementation of behavioural management programmes within a day treatment setting were described by Wood (1988). In any outpatient service there is only a limited amount of time actually spent in rehabilitation activities as opposed to mealtimes and breaks, and the effect of the daily change of environment between the home and the rehabilitation unit needs to be understood and managed appropriately. For example, there are usually different attitudes towards styles and extent of behaviour within these settings. The family may be seen as more permissive, condoning, and protective, thereby providing a less pressured environment, whereas the clinical setting is often perceived by the injured person (and family) as demanding and high-pressured. The contrast between these environments limits the consistency with which organisational strategies can be carried over to the patient's home. The extent to which family members can be expected to implement behavioural methods in a non-technical, non-threatening, and unpressured manner is determined by the extent to which the family understands the reasons for such treatment. This understanding is often limited and constrained by emotional issues and feelings of guilt.

Wood suggested that a "skills based" patient–family education programme could be used in conjunction with a method of behavioural contracting, to provide guidelines that a family could follow and which linked the activities of treatment staff with the role that relatives perform at home. He argued that the use of a behavioural contract could help social and functional aspects of behaviour generalise from the clinical setting to the home, and could give the family more confidence that they are working with the clinical team. However there are few studies that have explored the efficacy of explicitly engaging families in behavioural contracts with this client group.

One exception is that of McKinlay and Hickox (1988), who involved relatives in the rehabilitation of memory impairment and poor anger control. They designed a behavioural management programme in conjunction with assertiveness training to be implemented at home with the family as co-therapist. They argued that temper outbursts were a socially unskilled form of assertion and that acceptable assertiveness behaviour and other social skills should be taught to broaden the client's existing repertoire. These skills were summarised as easily remembered acronyms and worksheets were provided to structure homework assignments. The behavioural programme included identification of situations likely to trigger aggressive responses, teaching sensitivity to signals of increasing anger, and using relaxation procedures as an alternative response. Those who had difficulty generating or complying with alternative steps were encouraged to remove themselves from the anger-provoking situation. Records were kept of the brain-injured person's response in each situation and later reviewed. The co-therapist or relative participated in each treatment session (with the opportunity to meet separately with the therapist), and was provided with information summaries about their own responses to the client's problems, including advice on handling stressful situations.

Results were somewhat mixed in the study and McKinlay and Hickox discussed some of the obstacles to progress, focusing particularly on the emotional status of the relative involved. They concluded that while relatives may be effective co-workers in the late rehabilitation of memory and temper control deficits, therapists must be aware of and be able to handle the complexity of family relationships and expectations, including denial, guilt, and family roles.

What this study highlights is the difficulty of meeting the needs of the relative at the same time or in the same way as the needs of the injured person. The injured person and their relatives may be at very different stages in their adjustment to the situation, and at times their needs may conflict with negative effects on the rehabilitation process, as was the case for Sarah, a 32-year-old woman, who was living with her partner and a 2-year-old daughter at the time of injury. She was in a stationary vehicle that was struck by a lorry and she suffered a severe closed head injury. One year post-injury she had made a good physical recovery but suffered from cognitive problems particularly relating to attention. In particular, she was unable to divide her attention between two tasks successfully, for example, if she was changing the baby's nappy she would not hear the telephone ring. During a successful period of rehabilitation she learnt to organise and structure her activities, and to complete tasks requiring concentration within a quiet environment. Her partner, however, found it difficult to cooperate with this programme. He wanted to return to their previously spontaneous lifestyle and made frequent negative comparisons between her pre-injury level of functioning and what she could currently achieve. He was offered counselling and education. The benefits of the rehabilitation approach were demonstrated in practical terms repeatedly, but he was unable to acknowledge these positive changes. Whilst Sarah remained in this environment her potential to cope with the effects of her head injury was impaired. She was able to see how her partner's actions affected her progress, and her emotional turmoil was increased as she sought to balance her commitment to the relationship with her need to use rehabilitation strategies to cope with the demands of her child.

Behaviour management and family support

The interaction between the management of behaviour and the stages of family adjustment is a theme that runs through the literature on working with the families of people with brain injury. The acknowledgement that behavioural change is one of the greatest stresses has been coupled with the widespread recognition of the emotional demands made on family members who take on the long-term care role. This has produced a change in the approach to family support which does include within it more explicit descriptions of behaviours and attempts to identify appropriate interventions. There is a greater emphasis on training families to problem-solve for themselves. At the same time there is recognition that practical coping and emotional coping are parallel processes, and that if a family is to achieve some resolution to the trauma brought about by the injury to one of its members, then both processes need to be addressed.

There has been a development in the use of family therapy following brain injury but within this there has been an emphasis on the directive nature of therapy with this client group (Solomon & Scherzer, 1991). Guidelines for family therapists have described the use of logbooks, memory aids, visible reminders, and the role of routine and structure. Families have been encouraged to look at what is unacceptable behaviour and how they can tackle this. Family therapy has been used explicitly to develop methods for resolving conflicts within the relationship patterns of the family system (Rosenthal & Muir, 1983). They included homework assignments for the family to practise outside the sessions to foster generalisation of behaviour change. These assignments involved specific tasks that the family members were asked to perform between sessions to create desirable behavioural change.

Family therapy as it has developed with brain-injured patients has begun to bridge the gap between family counselling and family training, the primary difference between the two being that the latter has a more focused approach to the behavioural method of problem solving with specific objectives.

Behavioural family training

Behavioural family training has been defined as the establishment of specific operationalised goals and techniques for teaching family members to more effectively manage the problems presented by traumatic brain injury (Muir, Rosenthal, & Diehl, 1990). Muir et al. drew a parallel with other areas such as training communication and problem-solving skills to families of people with schizophrenia who relapse (Falloon et al., 1981), and teaching behaviour management skills to families of "acting out" children (Falloon & Liberman, 1976).

For families who prefer to "do" rather than "talk", a more direct behavioural training approach can be useful. The most thoroughly described model of behavioural family training for people with brain injury is that of Jacobs (1991). He argued that by emphasising problem-solving techniques and outcomes, rather than processes, the participants take a stronger role in the development of selected interventions and can more concretely measure their accomplishments by the progress they make on specific issues. He had previously argued (Jacobs 1989) that the nature of treatment following brain injury may facilitate the development of learned helplessness, in that patients and families are repeatedly presented with problems rather than solutions, and that they "learn" that they have no control over major events which affect their lives. They may become dependent, depressed, and passive. Jacobs' family training model, with explicit targets and successes, seeks to combat this sense of powerlessness.

The overall training model included the seven components of education, namely problem identification; problem selection; resource assessment; behavioural assessment; intervention; evaluation; and maintenance/generalisation. The majority of intervention strategies were usually fairly simple, once the controlling variables and their relationship to the targeted behaviour had been established. Interventions usually consisted of rearranging the environmental and interpersonal interactions to foster behavioural change. In many cases it was another family member, rather than the survivor, who had to make the adjustments. In other situations the survivor was asked to make significant changes in behaviour and to participate in planning and carrying out the intervention. Training in basic principles of reinforcement, stimulus control, and shaping techniques also helped families understand and work with motivational problems. Jacobs argues that families can learn the critical skills that can be applied to future problems as they develop, rather than placing the responsibility for and control of such processes with the therapist.

SUMMARY

Working with people who have sustained brain injury is difficult and demanding. Staff need appropriate training and support if they are to provide a high standard of care and input. Their interactions with relatives can be more effective and less stressful if staff are educated to understand the experience from the perspective of the relative as well as the patient.

There is widespread recognition of the role of families in rehabilitation, although the literature has focused primarily on the burden of care and level of distress experienced by these families. Support and education are recognised as essential parts of a rehabilitation service. There is a strong case for arguing that families should not become therapists as such, and that this should not be an expectation placed on families. Nevertheless, the majority of families want to be involved in the long-term care of their brain-injured relative, and in practice, many of them have little choice. While it is unrealistic to expect family members to maintain the consistency and intensity that many behavioural programmes require for long periods, it is often possible to institute less intrusive maintenance programmes.

If behavioural approaches are widely endorsed as useful management strategies for brain-injured adults, then there is a clear case for more training for staff and families in their use. The current implicit behavioural work that occurs during family education and support programmes should be made more explicit.

References

Alderman, N. (1991). The treatment of avoidance behaviour following severe brain injury by satiation through negative practice. *Brain Injury, 5*, 77–86.

Alderman, N. (1996). Central executive deficit and response to operant conditioning methods. *Neuropsychological Rehabilitation, 6*, 161–186.

Alderman, N. (2001). Management of challenging behaviour. In R. L. Wood & T. McMillan (Eds.), *Neurobehavioural disability and social handicap following traumatic brain injury* (pp. 175–207). Hove, UK: Psychology Press.

Alderman, N., & Burgess, P. W. (1990). Integrating cognition and behaviour: A pragmatic approach to brain injury rehabilitation. In R. L. Wood & I. Fussey (Eds.), *Cognitive rehabilitation in perspective* (pp. 204–228). New York: Taylor & Francis.

Alderman, N., Davies, J. A., Jones, C., & McDonnel, P. (1999). Reduction of severe aggressive behaviour in acquired brain injury: Case studies illustrating clinical use of the OAS-MNR in the management of challenging behaviours. *Brain Injury, 13*, 669–704.

Alderman, N., Fry, R. K., & Youngson, H. A. (1995). Improvement of self-monitoring skills, reduction of behaviour disturbance and the dysexecutive syndrome: Comparison of response cost and a new programme of self-monitoring training. *Neuropsychological Rehabilitation, 5*, 193–221.

Alderman, N., & Knight, C. (1997). The effectiveness of DRL in the management and treatment of severe behaviour disorders following brain injury. *Brain Injury, 11*(2), 79–101.

Alderman, N., Shepherd, J., & Youngson, H. (1992). Increasing standing tolerance and posture quality following severe brain injury using a behaviour modification approach. *Physiotherapy, 78*, 335–343.

Alderman, N., & Ward, A. (1991). Behavioural treatment of the dysexecutive syndrome: Reduction of repetitive speech using response cost and cognitive overlearning. *Neuropsychological Rehabilitation, 1*, 65–80.

Anastasi, A. (1988). *Psychological testing* (6th ed.). New York: Macmillan.

Andersson, S., Gundersen, P. M., & Finset, A. (1999). Emotional activation during therapeutic interaction in traumatic brain injury: Effect of apathy, self-awareness and implications for rehabilitation. *Brain Injury, 13*, 393–404.

Andrews, K., Murphy, L., Munday, R., & Littlewood, C. (1996). Misdiagnosis of the vegetative state—Retrospective study in a rehabilitation unit. *British Medical Journal, 313*, 13–16.

123

Anthony, M. V. (1999). Outline of a general methodology for consciousness research. *Anthropology and Philosophy*, *3*(2), 43–56.

Baddeley, A. D. (1999). *Essentials of human memory*. Hove, UK: Psychology Press.

Baddeley, A. D., & Hitch, G. (1974). Working memory. In G. H. Bower (Ed.), *The psychology of learning and motivation* (Vol. 8, pp. 47–89). New York: Academic Press.

Baddeley, A. D., & Longman, D. J. A. (1978). The influence of length and frequency on training sessions on the rate of learning to type. *Ergonomics*, *21*, 627–635.

Baddeley, A. D., & Wilson, B. A. (1994). When implicit learning fails: Amnesia and the problem of error elimination. *Neuropsychologia*, *32*, 53–68.

Bellus, S. B., Kost, P. P., Vergo, J. G., & Dinezza, G. J. (1998). Improvements in cognitive functioning following intensive behavioural rehabilitation. *Brain Injury*, *12*, 139–145.

Berrol, S. (1990). Persistent vegetative state. *Physical Medicine and Rehabilitation: State of the Art Reviews*, *4*, 559–576.

Blackerby, W. F. (1988). Practical token economies. *Journal of Head Trauma Rehabilitation*, *3*, 33–45.

Bluma, S., Shearer, M., Frohman, A., & Hilliard, J. (1976). *Portage guide to early education*. Wisconsin: Co-operative Educational Service Agency.

Booraem, C. D., & Seacat, G. F. (1972). Effects of increased incentive in corrective therapy. *Perceptual and Motor Skills*, *34*, 125–126.

Bowen, A., Chamberlain, M. A., Tennant, A., Neumann, V., & Conner, M. (1999). The persistence of mood disorders following traumatic brain injury: A one year follow up. *Brain Injury*, *13*, 547–553.

Bowen, A., Neumann, V., Conner, M., Tennant, A., & Chamberlain, M. A. (1998). Mood disorders following traumatic brain injury: Identifying the extent of the problem and the people at risk. *Brain Injury*, *12*, 177–190.

Braunling-McMorrow, D. (1994). Behavioural rehabilitation. In P. M. Deutsch & K. B. Frankish (Eds.), *Innovations in head injury rehabilitation*. New York: Mathew Bender.

Brooks, D. N., & Baddeley, A. D. (1976). What can amnesic patients learn? *Neuropsychologia*, *14*, 111–122.

Brooks, N., Campsie, L., Symington, C., Beattie, A., & McKinlay, W. (1986) The five year outcome of severe blunt head injury: A relative's view. *Journal of Neurology, Neurosurgery and Psychiatry*, *49*, 764–770.

Burgess, P. W., & Alderman, N. (1990). Rehabilitation of dyscontrol syndromes following frontal lobe damage: A cognitive neuropsychological approach. In R. L. Wood & I. Fussey (Eds.), *Cognitive rehabilitation in perspective* (pp. 183–203). New York: Taylor & Francis.

Burke, W. H., & Lewis, F. D. (1986). Management of maladaptive social behaviour of a brain-injured adult. *Rehabilitation Research*, *9*, 335–343.

Burke, W. H., Wesolowski, M. D., & Guth, W. L. (1988a). Comprehensive head injury rehabilitation: An outcome evaluation. *Brain Injury*, *2*, 313–322.

Burke, W. H., Wesolowski, M. D., & Lane, I. M. (1988b). A positive approach to the treatment of aggressive brain-injured clients. *International Journal of Rehabilitation Research*, *11*, 235–241.

Camp, C. J. (1989). Facilitation of new learning in Alzheimer's disease. In T. Gilmore, P. Whitehouse, & M. Wykle (Eds.), *Memory and aging: Theory research and practice* (pp. 212–225). New York: Springer.

Camp, C. J. (2001). From efficacy to effectiveness to diffusion: Making the transitions in dementia intervention research. *Neuropsychological Rehabilitation*, *11*, 495–517.

Camp, C. J., Bird, M., & Cherry, K. (2000). Retrieval strategies as a rehabilitation aid for cognitive loss in pathological aging. In R. D. Hill, L. Bäckman, & A. Stigsdotter-Neely (Eds.), *Cognitive rehabilitation in old age*. New York: Oxford University Press.

Camp, C. J., Foss, J. W., O'Hanlon, A. M., & Stevens, A. B. (1996). Memory interventions for persons with dementia. *Applied Cognitive Psychology*, *10*, 1193–1210.

Carberry, H. (1990). *How to be a really dysfunctional rehabilitation team* (pp. 4–6). New Jersey Rehabilitation.

Carr, S., & Wilson, B. A. (1983). Promotion of pressure relief exercising in a spinal injury patient: A multiple baseline across settings design. *Behavioural Psychotherapy, 11*, 329–336.

Cartlidge, N. (2001). States related to or confused with coma. *Journal of Neurology, Neurosurgery and Psychiatry, 71*, Suppl 1, 18–19.

Childs, N. L., Mercer, W. N., & Childs, H. W. (1993). Accuracy of diagnosis of persistent vegetative state. *Neurology, 43*, 1465–1467.

Clare, L., Wilson, B. A., Breen, E. K., & Hodges, J. R. (1999). Errorless learning of face–name associations in early Alzheimer's disease. *Neurocase, 5*, 37–46.

Clare, L., Wilson, B. A., Carter, G., Breen, E. K., Gosses, A., & Hodges, J. R. (2000). Intervening with everyday memory problems in dementia of Alzheimer type: An errorless learning approach. *Journal of Clinical and Experimental Neuropsychology, 22*, 132–146.

Clare, L., Wilson, B. A., Carter, G., Hodges, J. R., & Adams, M. (2001). Long-term maintenance of treatment gains following a cognitive rehabilitation intervention in early dementia of Alzheimer type: A single case study. *Neuropsychological Rehabilitation, 11*, 477–494.

Coltheart, M. (1985). Cognitive neuropsychology and reading. In M. Posner & O. S. M. Marin (Eds.), *Attention and performance XI* (pp. 3–37). Hillsdale, NJ: Lawrence Erlbaum Associates Inc.

Crosson, B., Barco, P. P., Velozo, C. A., Bolesta, M. M., Cooper, P. V., Werts, D. et al. (1989). Awareness and compensation in postacute head injury rehabilitation. *Journal of Head Trauma Rehabilitation, 4*, 46–54.

Cullen, C. N. (1976). Errorless learning with the retarded. *Nursing Times*, 25 March, 45–47.

Davies, W. (1989). The prevention of assault of professional helpers. In K. Howells & C. R. Hollin (Eds.), *Clinical approaches to violence* (pp. 311–328). Chichester, UK: John Wiley & Sons.

Diehl, L. N. (1983). Patient–family education. In M. Rosenthal, E. R. Griffith, M. R. Bond, & J. D. Miller (Eds.), *Rehabilitation of the head injured adult* (pp. 395–403). Philadelphia: F. A. Davis.

Diller, L. (1980). The development of a perceptual remediation program in hemiplegia. In L. P. Ince (Ed.), *Behavior psychology in rehabilitation medicine* (pp. 64–86). Baltimore, MD: Williams & Wilkins.

Diller, L. (1987). Neuropsychological rehabilitation. In M. J. Meier, A. L. Benton, & L. Diller (Eds.), *Neuropsychological rehabilitation* (pp. 3–17). Edinburgh: Churchill Livingstone.

Diller, L., & Weinberg, J. (1977). Hemi-inattention in rehabilitation: The evolution of a rational remediation program. In E. A. Weinstein & R. P. Friedland (Eds.), *Advances in neurology* (Vol. 18, pp. 63–82). New York: Raven Press.

Doll, E. A. (1953). *The measurement of social competence*. Minneapolis: Educational Publishers.

Eames, P. (1988). Behaviour disorders after severe head injury: Their nature and causes and strategies for management. *Journal of Head Trauma Rehabilitation, 3*, 1–6.

Eames, P., Haffey, W. J., & Cope, D. N. (1990). Treatment of behavioural disorders. In M. Rosenthal, E. R. Griffith, M. R. Bond, & J. D. Miller (Eds.), *Rehabilitation of the adult and child with traumatic brain injury* (2nd ed.) (pp. 410–432). Philadelphia: F. A. Davis.

Edgington, E. S. (1982). Nonparametric tests for single-subject multiple schedule experiments. *Behavioral Assessment, 4*, 83–91.

Ellis, A. W., Flude, B. M., & Young, A. W. (1987). Neglect dyslexia and the early visual processing of letters in words and nonwords. *Cognitive Neuropsychology, 4*, 439–464.

Evans, J. J. (1994). Physiotherapy as a clinical science: The role of single case research designs. *Physiotherapy Practice, 10*, 65–68.

Evans, J. J. (2001). Rehabilitation of the dysexecutive syndrome. In R. L. Wood & T. McMillan (Eds.), *Neurobehavioural disability and social handicap* (pp. 209–227). Hove, UK: Psychology Press.

Evans, J. J., Emslie, H., & Wilson, B. A. (1998). External cueing systems in the rehabilitation of executive impairments of action. *Journal of the International Neuropsychological Society*, *4*, 399–408.

Evans, J. J., & Wilson, B. A. (1992). A memory group for individuals with brain injury. *Clinical Rehabilitation*, *6*, 75–81.

Eysenck, H. J. (1959). Learning theory and behaviour therapy. *Journal of Mental Science*, *105*, 61–75.

Falloon, I. R. H., & Liberman, R. (1976). Behaviour therapy for families with child management problems. In I. R. H. Falloon et al. (Eds.), *Families with child management problems*. New York: Plenum Press.

Falloon, I. R. H., et al. (1981). Family therapy with relapsing schizophrenics and their families: A pilot study. *Family Process*, *15*, 94.

Feeney, T. J., & Ylvisaker, M. (1995). Choice and routine: Antecedent behavioural interventions for adolescents with severe traumatic brain injury. *Journal of Head Trauma Rehabilitation*, *10*, 67–86.

Feinstein, A. (1999). Mood and motivation in rehabilitation. In D. T. Stuss, G. Winocur, & I. H. Robertson (Eds.), *Cognitive neurorehabilitation* (pp. 230–239). New York: Cambridge University Press.

Finger, S., & Stein, D. G. (1982). *Brain damage and recovery: Research and clinical perspectives*. New York: Academic Press.

Fleminger, S., & Powell, J. (Eds.). (1999). *Neuropsychological Rehabilitation. Special Issue: Evaluation of outcomes in brain injury rehabilitation*. Hove, UK: Psychology Press.

Fonagy, P., Moran, G. S., & Higgitt, A. C. (1989). Hypertension. In S. Pearce & J. Wardle (Eds.), *The practice of behavioural medicine* (pp. 161–190). Oxford: BPS Books and Oxford University Press.

Foster, K. (1988). The role of behaviour management programs in the rehabilitation process. *Cognitive Rehabilitation*, *January/February*, 16–19.

Foxx, R. M., Marchand-Martella, N. E., Martella, R. C., Braunling-McMorrow, D., & McMorrow, M. J. (1988). Teaching a problem solving strategy to closed head injured adults. *Behavioural Residential Treatment*, *3*, 193–210.

Foxx, R. M., Martella, R. C., & Marchand-Martella, N. E. (1989). The acquisition, maintenance, and generalization of problem solving skills by closed head-injured adults. *Behaviour Therapy*, *20*, 61–76.

Franks, C. M., & Wilson, G. T. (1975). *Annual review of behaviour therapy: Theory and practice, 3*. New York: Brunner/Mazel.

Gainotti, G. (1993). Emotional and psychosocial problems after brain injury. *Neuropsychological Rehabilitation*, *3*, 259–277.

Gajar, A., Schloss, P. J., Schloss, C. N., & Thompson, C. K. (1984). Effects of feedback and self-monitoring on head trauma youths' conversation skills. *Journal of Applied Behaviour Analysis*, *17*, 353–358.

Garske, G. G., & Thomas, K. R. (1992). Self-reported self-esteem and depression: Indexes of psychosocial adjustment following severe traumatic brain injury. *Rehabilitation Counselling Bulletin*, *36*, 33–52.

Gianutsos, R., & Gianutsos, J. (1987). Single case experimental approaches to the assessment of interventions in rehabilitation psychology. In B. Caplan (Ed.), *Rehabilitation psychology* (pp. 453–470). Rockville, MD: Aspen Corp.

Gill-Thwaites, H., & Munday, R. (1999). The Sensory Modality Assessment and Rehabilitation Technique (SMART)—A comprehensive and integrated assessment and treatment protocol for the vegetative state and minimally responsive patient. *Neuropsychological Rehabilitation*, *9*, 305–320.

Glisky, E. L. (1995). Acquisition and transfer of word processing skill by an amnesic patient. *Neuropsychological Rehabilitation*, *5*, 299–318.

Glisky, E. L., & Schacter, D. L. (1987). Acquisition of domain-specific knowledge in organic amnesia: Training for computer-related work. *Neuropsychologia*, *25*, 893–906.

Glisky, E. L., Schacter, D. L., & Tulving, E. (1986). Computer learning by memory impaired patients: Acquisition and retention of complex knowledge. *Neuropsychologia*, *24*, 313–328.

Goodkin, R. (1966). Case studies in behavioral research in rehabilitation. *Perceptual and Motor Skills*, *23*, 171–182.

Goodkin, R. (1969). Changes in word production, sentence production and relevance in an aphasic through verbal conditioning. *Behaviour Research and Therapy*, *7*, 93–99.

Goodman-Smith, A., & Turnbull, J. (1983). A behavioural approach to the rehabilitation of severely brain-injured adults. *Physiotherapy*, *69*, 393–396.

Graf, P., & Schacter, D. L. (1985). Implicit and explicit memory for new associations in normal and amnesic subjects. *Journal of Experimental Psychology: Learning, Memory and Cognition*, *11*, 501–518.

Greif, E., & Matarazzo, R. G. (1982). *Behavioural approaches to rehabilitation: Coping with change* (pp. 110–115). New York: Springer Publishing Company.

Hagen, C., Malkmus, D., & Durham, P. (1987). Levels of cognitive functioning. In Professional Staff Association of Rancho Los Amigos Hospital (Eds.), *Rehabilitation of the head injured adult: Comprehensive physical management*. Downey, CA: Rancho Los Amigos Hospital Inc.

Halstead, W. C. (1947). *Brain and intelligence*. Chicago: University of Chicago Press.

Hegel, M. T., & Ferguson, R. J. (2000). Differential reinforcement of other behaviour (DRO) to reduce aggressive behaviour following traumatic brain injury. *Behaviour Modification*, *24*, 94–101.

Hegel, T. (1988). Application of a token economy with a non-compliant closed head injured male. *Brain Injury*, *2*, 333–378.

Hemsley, R., & Carr, J. (1980). Ways of increasing behaviour-reinforcement. In W. Yule & J. Carr (Eds.), *Behavioural modification for the mentally handicapped* (pp. 33–47). London: Croom Helm.

Herbert, C. M., & Powell, G. E. (1989). Insight and progress in rehabilitation. *Clinical Rehabilitation*, *3*, 125–130.

Hersen, M., & Barlow, D. H. (1976). *Single case experimental designs: Strategies for studying behavior change*. Elmsford, NY: Pergamon Press.

Holland, A. L. (1980). *CADL, Communicative Abilities in Daily Living: A test of functional communication for aphasic adults*. Baltimore, MD: University Park Press.

Horn, L. J., & Zasler, N. D. (1990). Neuroanatomy and neurophysiology of sexual function. *Journal of Head Trauma Rehabilitation*, *5*, 1–13.

Horn, S., Shiel, A., McLellan, D. L., Campbell, M., Watson, M., & Wilson, B. A. (1993). A review of behavioural assessment scales for monitoring recovery in and after coma with pilot data on a new scale of visual awareness. *Neuropsychological Rehabilitation*, *3*, 121–137.

Houts, P. S., & Scott, R. A. (1975). *Goal planning with developmentally disabled persons: Procedures for developing an individualized client plan*. Hershey, PA: Department of Behavioral Science, Pennsylvania State University College of Medicine.

Howard, M. E. (1988). Behaviour management in the acute care rehabilitation setting. *Journal of Head Trauma Rehabilitation*, *3*, 14–22.

Hunkin, M. M., Squires, E. J., Parkin, A. J., & Tidy, J. A. (1998). Are the benefits of errorless learning dependent on implicit memory? *Neuropsychologia*, *36*, 25–36.

I Fortuny, L. A., Briggs, M., Newcombe, F., Ratcliffe, G., & Thomas, C. (1980). Measuring the duration of post traumatic amnesia. *Journal of Neurology, Neurosurgery and Psychiatry*, *43*, 377–379.

Ince, L. P. (1976). *Behavior modification in rehabilitation medicine.* Baltimore: Williams & Wilkins.

Ince, L. P. (1980). *Behavior psychology in rehabilitation medicine.* Baltimore: Williams & Wilkins.

Jackson, W. T., & Gouvier, W. D. (1992). Group psychotherapy with brain-damaged adults and their families. In C. J. Long & L. K. Ross (Eds.), *Handbook of head trauma: Acute care to recovery.* New York: Plenum Press.

Jacobs, H. (1989). Long-term family intervention. In D. W. Ellis & A.-L. Christensen (Eds.), *Neuropsychological treatment after brain injury* (pp. 297–316). Boston: Kluver.

Jacobs, H. (1991). Family and behavioural issues. In J. M. Williams & T. Kay (Eds.), *Head injury: A family matter.* Baltimore: Paul H. Brookes.

Jacobs, H. E., Lynch, M., Cornick, J., & Slifer, K. (1986). Behaviour management of aggressive sequelae after Reye's syndrome. *Archives of Physical Medicine and Rehabilitation, 67,* 558–563.

Jennett, B., & Plum, F. (1972). Persistent vegetative state after head injury: A syndrome in search of a name. *Lancet, i,* 734–737.

Jennett, B., & Teasdale, G. (1977). Aspects of coma after severe head injury. *The Lancet, i,* 878–881.

Johnston, D., & Steptoe, A. (1989). Hypertension. In S. Pearce & J. Wardle (Eds.), *The practice of behavioural medicine* (pp. 1–25). Oxford: BPS Books and Oxford University Press.

Jones, R. S. P., & Eayrs, C. B. (1992). The use of errorless learning procedures in teaching people with a learning disability. *Mental Handicap Research, 5,* 304–312.

Katz, D. I. (1992). Neuropathology and neurobehavioural recovery from closed head injury. *Journal of Head Trauma Rehabilitation, 7,* 1–15.

Kazdin, A. (1980). *Research design in clinical psychology.* New York: Harper & Row.

Kazdin, A. E. (1978). *History of behavior modification: Experimental foundations of contemporary research.* Baltimore, MD: University Park Press.

Kazdin, A. E. (1982). *Single-case research designs: Methods for clinical and applied settings.* New York: Oxford University Press.

Kazdin, A. E., & Hersen, M. (1980). The current status of behaviour therapy. *Behaviour Modification, 4,* 283–302.

Kopelman, M., & Crawford, S. (1996). Not all memory clinics are dementia clinics. *Neuropsychological Rehabilitation, 6,* 187–202.

Kopelman, M., Wilson, B. A., & Baddeley, A. D. (1990). *The Autobiographical Memory Interview.* Bury St Edmunds, UK: Thames Valley Test Company.

Kozloff, R. (1987). Network of social support and the outcome from severe head injury. *Journal of Head Trauma Rehabilitation, 2,* 14–23.

Kratochwill, T. R. (1978). *Single subject research: Strategies for evaluating change.* New York: Academic Press.

Kreutzer, J. S., Gervasio, A. H., & Camplair, P. S. (1994). Primary caregivers' psychological status and family functioning after traumatic brain injury. *Brain Injury, 8,* 197–210.

Kreutzer, J. S., & Zasler, N. D. (1989). Psychosexual consequences of traumatic brain injury: Methodology and preliminary findings. *Brain Injury, 3,* 177–186.

Landauer, T. K., & Bjork, R. A. (1978). Optimum rehearsal patterns and name learning. In M. M. Gruneberg, P. E. Morris, & R. N. Sykes (Eds.), *Practical aspects of memory* (pp. 625–632). London: Academic Press.

Lane, H. (1977). *The wild boy of Aveyron.* London: Paladin-Granada.

Langer, K. G., & Padrone, F. J. (1992) Psychotherapeutic treatment of awareness in acute rehabilitation of traumatic brain injury. *Neuropsychological Rehabilitation, 2,* 59–70.

Langosch, W. (1989). Cardiac rehabilitation. In S. Pearce & J. Wardle (Eds.), *The practice of behavioural medicine* (pp. 27–49). Oxford: BPS Books and Oxford University Press.

Lavender, A. (1981). A behavioural approach to the treatment of epilepsy. *Behavioural Psychotherapy, 9,* 231–243.

Lazarus, A. A. (1971). *Behavior therapy and beyond.* New York: McGraw-Hill.

Levenkron, J. C. (1987). Behavior modification in rehabilitation medicine: Principles and clinical strategies. In B. Caplan (Ed.), *Rehabilitation psychology desk reference* (pp. 383–416). Rockville, MD: Aspen Publishers, Inc.

Levin, H. S., High, W. M., Goethe, K. E., Sisson, R. A., Overall, J. E., Rhoades, H. M. et al. (1987) The Neurobehavioural Rating Scale: Assessment of the behavioural sequelae of head injury by the clinician. *Journal of Neurology, Neurosurgery and Psychiatry, 50*, 183–193.

Levin, H. S., O'Donnell, V. M., & Grossman, R.G. (1979). The Galveston Orientation and Amnesia Test. *Journal of Nervous and Mental Disease, 167*, 657–684.

Levine, J., & Zigler, E. (1975). Denial and self image in stroke, lung cancer, and heart disease patients. *Journal of Consulting and Clinical Psychology, 43*, 751–757.

Lewis, F. D., Nelson, J., Nelson, C., & Reusink, P. (1988). Effects of three feedback contingencies on the socially inappropriate talk of a brain-injured adult. *Behaviour Therapy, 19*, 203–211.

Lezak, M. D. (1987). Living with the characteriologically altered brain injured patient. *Journal of Clinical Psychiatry, 34*, 592–598.

Lezak, M. (1995). *Neuropsychological assessment* (3rd ed.). New York: Oxford University Press.

Lincoln, N. B. (1978). Behaviour modification in physiotherapy. *Physiotherapy, 64*, 265–267.

Lincoln, N. B., & Pickersgill, M. J. (1984). An evaluation of programmed instruction in the language rehabilitation of severe aphasics. *Behavioural Psychotherapy, 12*, 237–248.

Lincoln, N. B., Pickersgill, M. J., Hankey, A. I., & Hilton, C. R. (1982). An evaluation of operant training and speech therapy in the language rehabilitation of moderate aphasics. *Behavioural Psychotherapy, 10*, 162–178.

Lira, F. T., Carne, W., & Masri, A. M. (1983). Treatment of anger and impulsivity in a brain damaged patient: A case study applying stress inoculation. *Clinical Neuropsychology, 5*, 159–160.

Livingston, M. G., & Brooks, D. N. (1988). The burden on families of the brain injured: A review. *Journal of Head Trauma Rehabilitation, 3*, 6–15.

Luria, A. R. (1963). *Restoration of function after brain injury.* New York: Pergamon Press.

Luria, A. R., Naydin, V. L., Tsvetkova, L. S., & Vinarskaya, E. N. (1969). Restoration of higher cortical functions following local brain damage. In P. J. Vinken & G. W. Bruyn (Eds.), *Handbook of clinical neurology* (Vol. 3, pp. 368–433). New York: Elsevier.

Lysaght, R., & Bodenheimer, E. (1990). The use of relaxation training to enhance functional outcomes in adults with traumatic head injuries. *American Journal of Occupational Therapy, 44*, 797–802.

Malec, J. (1984). Training the brain-injured client in behavioural self-management skills. In B. A. Edelstein & E. T. Couture (Eds.), *Behaviour assessment and rehabilitation of traumatically brain damaged adults* (pp. 121–150). New York. Plenum Press.

Martin, P. R. (Ed.). (1991). *Handbook of behavior therapy and psychological science: An integrative approach. Pergamon general psychology series, Vol. 164* (pp. 227–252). Elmsford, NY: Pergamon Press, Inc.

McGlynn, S. M., & Schacter, D. L. (1989). Unawareness of deficits in neuropsychological syndromes. *Journal of Clinical and Experimental Neuropsychology, 11*, 143–205.

McGrath, J. (1997). Cognitive impairment associated with post-traumatic stress disorder and minor head injury: A case report. *Neuropsychological Rehabilitation, 7*, 231–239.

McKinlay, W. W., Brooks, D. N., Bond, M. R., Martinage, D. P., & Marshall, M. M. (1981). The short-term outcome of severe blunt head injury as reported by relatives of the injured persons. *Journal of Neurology, Neurosurgery and Psychiatry, 44*, 527–533.

McKinlay, W. W., & Hickox, A. (1988). How can families help in the rehabilitation of the head injured? *Journal of Head Trauma Rehabilitation, 3*, 64–72.

McMillan, T., & Sparkes, C. (1999). Goal planning and neurorehabilitation: The Wolfson Neurorehabilitation Centre approach. *Neuropsychological Rehabilitation, 9*, 241–251.

McMillan, T. M. (1991). Posttraumatic stress disorder and severe head injury. *British Journal of Psychiatry, 159*, 431–433.

McMillan, T. M. (1996). Posttraumatic stress disorder following minor and severe closed head injury: 10 single cases. *Brain Injury, 10,* 749–758.

McMillan, T. M., Jongen, E. L., & Greenwood, R. J. (1996). Assessment of post-traumatic amnesia after severe closed head injury: Retrospective or prospective? *Journal of Neurology, Neurosurgery and Psychiatry, 60,* 422–427.

McMillan, T. M., Papadopoulos, H., Cornall, C., & Greenwood, R. J. (1990). Modification of severe behaviour problems following herpes simplex encephalitis. *Brain Injury, 4,* 399–406.

Melin, L., Sjödén, P.-O., & James, J. E. (1983). Neurological impairments. In M. Hersen, V. B. van Hasselt, & J. L. Matson (Eds.), *Behavior therapy for the developmentally and physically disabled* (pp. 267–306). New York: Academic Press.

Meyerson, L., Kerr, N., & Michael, J. L. (1967). Behaviour modification in rehabilitation. In S. W. Bijou & D. M. Baer (Eds.), *Child development: Readings in experimental analysis* (pp. 214–239). New York: Appleton Century Crofts.

Miller, E. (1980). Psychological intervention in the management and rehabilitation of neuropsychological impairments. *Behavioural Research and Therapy, 18,* 527–535.

Miller, E. (1984). *Recovery and management of neuropsychological impairments.* Chichester, UK: John Wiley & Sons.

Miller, L. (1993). The "trauma" of head traumas: Clinical, neuropsychological, and forensic aspects of posttraumatic stress syndromes in brain injury. *Journal of Cognitive Rehabilitation, 11,* 18–29.

Moffat, N. (1989). Home based cognitive rehabilitation with the elderly. In L. W. Poon, D. C. Rubin, & B. A. Wilson (Eds.), *Everyday cognition in adulthood and late life* (pp. 659–680). Cambridge: Cambridge University Press.

Morley, S., & Adams, M. (1989). Some simple statistics for exploring single-case time series data. *British Journal of Clinical Psychology, 28,* 1–18.

Muir, C. A., Rosenthal, M., & Diehl, L. N. (1990). Methods of family intervention. In M. Rosenthal, E. R. Griffith, & C. R. Bond (Eds.), *Rehabilitation of the adult and child with traumatic brain injury* (2nd ed.) (pp. 433–448). Philadelphia: F. A. Davis.

Murphy, G., & Oliver, C. (1987). Decreasing undesirable behaviour. In W. Yule & J. Carr (Eds.), *Behaviour modification for people with mental handicaps* (2nd ed., pp. 102–142). London: Croom Helm.

Novack, T. A., Bergquist, T. F., & Bennett, G. (1992). Family involvement in cognitive recovery following traumatic brain injury. In C. J. Long & L. K. Ross (Eds.), *Handbook of head trauma: Acute care to recovery* (pp. 329–355). New York: Plenum Press.

O'Leary, C. A. (2000). Reducing aggression in adults with brain injuries. *Behavioural Interventions, 15,* 205–216.

Oddy, M., Humphrey, M., & Uttley, D. (1978). Stresses upon the relatives of head injured patients. *British Journal of Psychiatry, 133,* 507–513.

Page, M., Wilson, B. A., Norris, D., Shiel, A., & Carter, G. (2001). Familiarity and recollection in errorless learning. *Journal of the International Neuropsychological Society, 7,* 413 (abstract).

Patterson, K. (1994). Reading, writing and rehabilitation: A reckoning. In M. J. Riddoch & G. W. Humphrey (Eds.), *Cognitive neuropsychology and cognitive rehabilitation* (pp. 425–447). Hove, UK: Lawrence Erlbaum Associates Ltd.

Patterson, K. E., & Wilson, B. A. (1990). A ROSE is a ROSE or a NOSE: A deficit in initial letter identification. *Cognitive Neuropsychology, 7,* 447–477.

Pearce, S., & Wardle, J. (Eds.). (1989). *The practice of behavioural medicine.* Oxford: Oxford University Press.

Peters, M. D., Gluck, M., & McCormick, M. (1992). Behaviour rehabilitation of the challenging client in less restrictive settings. *Brain Injury, 6,* 299–314.

Plum, F., & Posner, J. B. (1980). *The diagnosis of stupor and coma* (3rd ed.). Philadelphia: F. A. Davis.

Possl, J., Jurgensmeyer, S., Karlbauer, F., Wenz, C., & Goldenberg, G. (2001). Stability of employment after brain injury: A 7-year follow up study. *Brain Injury*, *15*, 15–27.

Powell, G. E. (1981). *Brain function therapy*. Aldershot, UK: Gower Press.

Powell, G. E. (1986). The self after brain injury: Theory, research and rehabilitation. *Journal of Clinical and Experimental Neuropsychology*, *8*, 115.

Prigatano, G. P. (1995). Personality and social aspects of memory rehabilitation. In A. D. Baddeley, B. A. Wilson, & F. N. Watts (Eds.), *Handbook of memory disorders* (pp. 603–614). Chichester, UK: John Wiley & Sons.

Prigatano, G. P. (2000). Rehabilitation for traumatic brain injury. *The Journal of the American Medical Association*, *284*, 1783.

Prigatano, G. P., Fordyce, D. J., Zeiner, H. K., Roueche, J. R., Pepping, M., & Wood, B. C. (1986). Neuropsychological rehabilitation after closed head injury in young adults. *Journal of Neurology, Neurosurgery and Psychiatry*, *47*, 505–513.

Rappaport, M., Dougherty, A. M., & Kelting, D. L. (1992). Evaluation of coma and vegetative state. *Archives of Physical Medicine and Rehabilitation*, *73*, 628–634.

Rappaport, M., Hall, K. M., Hopkins, K., Belleza, T., Cope, N. (1982). Disability rating scale for severe head trauma: Coma to community. *Archives of Physical Medicine and Rehabilitation*, *63*, 118–123.

Reitan, R. M., & Davison, L. A. (1974). *Clinical neuropsychology: Current status and applications*. New York: Hemisphere.

Riddoch, M. J. (Ed.). (1991). *Neglect and the peripheral dyslexias: A special issue of the journal "Cognitive Neuropsychology"*. Hove, UK: Lawrence Erlbaum Associates Ltd.

Riddoch, M. J., & Humphries, G. W. (1994). Towards an understanding of neglect. In M. J. Riddoch & G. W. Humphries (Eds.), *Cognitive neuropsychology and cognitive rehabilitation* (pp. 125–149). Hove, UK: Lawrence Erlbaum Associates Ltd.

Rimm, D. C., & Masters, J. C. (1979). *Behavior therapy: Techniques and empirical findings* (2nd ed.). New York: Academic Press.

Robertson, I. H., Ward, T., Ridgeway, V., & Nimmo-Smith, I. (1994). *The Test of Everyday Attention*. Bury St Edmunds, UK: Thames Valley Test Company.

Rosenberg, J., Ashwal, S. (1996). Recent advances in the development of practice parameters: The vegetative state. *Neurorehabilitation*, *6*, 79–87.

Rosenthal, M., & Muir, C. A. (1983). Methods of family intervention. In M. Rosenthal, E. Griffith, M. Bond, & J. D. Miller (Eds.), *Rehabilitation of the head injured adult*. Philadelphia: FA Davis.

Rothwell, N. A., LaVigna, G. W., & Willis, T. J. (1999). A non-aversive rehabilitation approach for people with severe behavioural problems resulting from brain injury. *Brain Injury*, *13*, 521–533.

Royal College of Physicians (1996). The permanent vegetative state: Review of a Working Party convened by the Royal College of Physicians and endorsed by the Conference of Medical Royal Colleges and their faculties of the United Kingdom. *Journal of the Royal College of Physicians London*, *30*, 119–121.

Russell, W. R., & Nathan, P. W. (1946). Traumatic amnesia. *Brain*, *69*, 280–300.

Sander, A. M., Kreutzer, J. F., Rosenthal, M., Delmonico, R., & Young, M. E. (1996). A multicentre longitudinal investigation of return to work and community integration following traumatic brain injury. *Journal of Head Trauma Rehabilitation*, *11*, 70–84.

Sargent, M. M. (1989). Residential treatment. In D. W. Ellis & A.-L. Christensen (Eds.), *Neuropsychological treatment after brain injury*. Boston: Kluwer Academic Publishers.

Sbordone, R. J. (1988). Assessment and treatment of cognitive-communicative impairments in the closed head injury patient: A neurobehavioural-systems approach. *Journal of Head Trauma Rehabilitation*, *3*, 55–62.

Schacter, D. L., & Glisky, E. L. (1986). Memory remediation: Restoration, alleviation and the acquisition of domain-specific knowledge. In B. Uzzell & Y. Gross (Eds.), *Clinical neuropsychology of intervention* (pp. 257–282). Boston: Martinus Nijhoff.

Schacter, D. L., Rich, S. A., & Stampp, M. S. (1985). Remediation of memory disorders: Experimental evaluation of the spaced-retrieval technique. *Journal of Clinical and Experimental Neuropsychology*, 7, 79–96.

Schloss, P. J., Thompson, C. K., Gajar, A. H., & Schloss, C. N. (1985). Influence of self-monitoring on heterosexual conversational behaviours of head trauma youth. *Applied Research in Mental Retardation*, 6, 269–282.

Series, C., & Lincoln, N. B. (1978). Behaviour modification in physical rehabilitation. *British Journal of Occupational Therapy*, 41, 222–224.

Shiel, A., Horn, S. A., Wilson, B. A., Watson, M. J., Campbell, M., & McLellan, D. L. (2000a). The Wessex Head Injury Matrix (WHIM) main scale: A preliminary report on a scale to assess and monitor patient recovery after severe head injury. *Clinical Rehabilitation*; 14(4), 408–416.

Shiel, A., Wilson, B. A., McLellan, L., Horn, S., & Watson, M. (2000b). *The Wessex Head Injury Matrix (WHIM)*. Bury St Edmunds, UK: Thames Valley Test Company.

Sidman, M., & Stoddard, L. T. (1967). The effectiveness of fading in programming simultaneous form discrimination for retarded children. *Journal of Experimental Analysis of Behavior*, 10, 3–15.

Singh, N. N., Beale, I. L., & Dawson, M. (1981). Duration of facial screening and suppression of self-injurious behavior: Analysis using an alternating treatment design. *Behavioral Assessments*, 3, 411–420.

Slifer, K., Cataldo, M. D., & Kurtz, P. F. (1995). Behavioural training during acute brain trauma rehabilitation: An empirical case study. *Brain Injury*, 9, 585–593.

Sobell, M. B., & Sobell, L. C. (1978). Assessment of addictive behavior. In M. Hersen & A. S. Bellack (Eds.), *Behavioral assessment: A practical handbook* (pp. 305–336). Oxford: Pergamon Press.

Solomon, C., & Scherzer, P. (1991). Some guidelines for family therapists working with the traumatically brain injured and their families. *Brain Injury*, 5, 253–266.

Sparadeo, F. R., Strauss, D., & Barth, J. T. (1990). The incidence, impact, and treatment of substance abuse in head trauma rehabilitation. *Journal of Head Trauma Rehabilitation*, 5, 1–8.

Squires, E. J., Aldrich, F. K., Parkin, A. J., & Hunkin, N. M. (1998). Errorless learning and the acquisition of word processing skills. *Neuropsychological Rehabilitation*, 8, 433–449.

Squires, E. J., Hunkin, N. M., & Parkin, A. J. (1996). Memory notebook training in a case of severe amnesia: Generalising from paired associate learning to real life. *Neuropsychological Rehabilitation*, 6, 55–65.

Squires, E. J., Hunkin, N. M., & Parkin, A. J. (1997). Errorless learning of novel associations in amnesia. *Neuropsychologia*, 35, 1103–1111.

Stern, J. M., Sazbon, M. D., Becker, E., & Costeff, H. (1988) Severe behavioural disturbance in families of patients with prolonged coma. *Brain Injury*, 2, 259–262.

Sundberg, N. S., & Tyler, L. E. (1962). *Clinical psychology*. New York: Appleton-Century-Crofts.

Talbott, R. (1989). The brain injured person and the family. In R. L. Wood & P. Eames (Eds.), *Models of brain injury rehabiltiation* (pp. 3–16). London: Chapman & Hall.

Tate, R. L. (1987). Behaviour management techniques for organic psychosocial deficit incurred by severe head injury. *Scandinavian Journal of Rehabilitation Medicine*, 19, 19–24.

Taylor, G. P. J., & Persons, R. W. (1970). Behavior modification techniques in a physical medicine and rehabilitation center. *Journal of Psychology*, 74, 117–124.

Teasdale, T. W., & Engberg, A. W. (2001). Suicide after traumatic brain injury: A population study. *Journal of Neurology, Neurosurgery, and Psychiatry*, 71, 436–440.

Teasdale, G., & Jennett, B. (1974). Assessment of coma and impaired consciousness: A practical scale. *The Lancet*, 2, 81–84.

Terrace, H. S. (1963). Discrimination learning with and without "errors". *Journal of Experimental Analysis of Behavior*, 6, 1–27.

Terrace, H. S. (1966). Stimulus control. In W. K. Honig (Ed.), *Operant behavior: Areas of research and application* (pp. 271–344). New York: Appleton-Century-Crofts.

Thomsen, I. V. (1984). Late outcome of very severe blunt head trauma. A 10–15 year second follow up. *Journal of Neurology, Neurosurgery and Psychiatry, 46*, 870–875.

Thornton, S. (1989). Irritable bowel syndrome. In S. Pearce & J. Wardle (Eds.), *The practice of behavioural medicine* (pp. 223–254). Oxford: BPS Books and Oxford University Press.

Tsoi, M., & Yule, W. (1980). Building up new behaviours—shaping, prompting and fading. In W. Yule & J. Carr (Eds.), *Behaviour modification for the mentally handicapped*. London: Croom Helm.

Tulving, E., & Schacter, D. L. (1990). Priming and human memory systems. *Science, 247*, 301–306.

Turner, J. M., Green, G., & Braunling-McMorrow, D. (1990). Differential reinforcement of low fates of responding to reduce dysfunctional social behaviours of a head injured man. *Behavioural Residential Treatment, 5*, 15–27.

Walsh, B. F., & Lamberts, F. (1979). Errorless discrimination and fading as techniques for teaching sight words to TMR students. *American Journal of Mental Deficiency, 83*, 473–479.

Wang, P. L., & Ennis, K. E. (1986). Competency assessments in clinical populations: An introduction to the cognitive competency test. In B. P. Uzzell & Y. Gross (Eds.), *Clinical neuropsychology of intervention* (pp. 119–134). Boston: Martinus Nijhoff.

Warden, D. L., Labbate, L. A., Salazar, A. M., Nelson, R., Sheley, E., Staudenmeier, J. et al. (1997). Posttraumatic stress disorder in patients with traumatic brain injury and amnesia for the event? *Journal of Neuropsychiatry and Clinical Neurosciences, 9*, 18–22.

Warrington, E. K., & James, M. (1991). *The Visual Object and Space Perception Battery*. Bury St Edmunds, UK: Thames Valley Test Company.

Watson, M., & Horn, S. (1991). The ten-pound note test: Suggestions for eliciting improved reponses in the severely brain injured patient. *Brain Injury, 5*, 421–424.

Watson, M., Horn, S., Wilson, B. A., Shiel, A., & McLellan, D. L. (1997). The application of a paired comparison technique to identify sequence of recovery after severe head injury. *Neuropsychological Rehabilitation, 7*, 441–458.

Webster, G., Daisley, A., & King, N. (1999). Relationship and family breakdown following acquired brain injury: The role of the rehabilitation team. *Brain Injury, 13*, 593–603.

Wechsler, D. (1981). *Wechsler Adult Intelligence Scale—Revised*. New York: The Psychological Corporation.

Wechsler, D. (1987). *The Wechsler Memory Scale—Revised*. San Antonio, CA: The Psychological Corporation.

Weinberg, J., Diller, L., Gordon, W. A., Gerstman, L. J., Lieberman, A., Lakin, P. et al. (1979). Training sensory awareness and spatial organization in people with right brain damage. *Archives of Physical Medicine and Rehabilitation, 60*, 491–496.

Weinstein, E. A. (1991). Anosognosia and denial of illness. In G. P. Prigatano & D. L. Schacter (Eds.), *Awareness of deficit after brain injury: Clinical and theoretical issues* (pp. 240–257). New York: Oxford University Press.

Weinstein, E. N., & Kahn, R. L. (1950). The syndrome of anosagnosia. *Archives of General Psychiatry, 64*, 772–791.

Williams, H. W., Evans, J. J., & Wilson, B. A. (2000). *Obsessive compulsive disorder after brain injury. Cognitive behaviour therapy in neurorehabilitation: A case illustration*. Paper presented at The British Association of Behaviour and Cognitive Psychotherapies Annual Conference, Institute of Education, London.

Williams, H. W., Evans, J. J., & Wilson, B. A. (2003). Neurorehabilitation for post traumatic stress disorder for two survivors of traumatic brain injury. *Clinical Neuropsychiatry, 8*, 1–18.

Williams, H. W., Evans, J. J., Wilson, B. A., & Needham, P. (2002). Prevalence of post-traumatic stress disorder symptoms after severe traumatic brain injury in a representative community sample. *Brain Injury, 16*, 673–679.

Wilson, B. A. (1981). A survey of behavioural treatments carried out at a rehabilitation centre. In G. Powell (Ed.), *Brain function therapy* (pp. 256–275). Aldershot, UK: Gower Press.

Wilson, B. A. (1985). Adapting "portage" for neurological patients. *International Rehabilitation Medicine*, *7*, 6–8.

Wilson, B. A. (1987). Single-case experimental designs in neuropsychological rehabilitation. *Journal of Clinical and Experimental Neuropsychology*, *9*, 527–544.

Wilson, B. A. (1988). Future directions in rehabilitation of brain injured people. In A.-L. Christensen & B. Uzzell (Eds.), *Neuropsychological rehabilitation* (pp. 69–86). Boston: Kluwer Academic Publishers.

Wilson, B. A. (1989). Management of problems resulting from damage to the central nervous system. In S. Pearce & J. Wardle (Eds.), *The practice of behavioural medicine* (pp. 51–81). Oxford: Oxford University Press.

Wilson, B. A. (1991a). Theory, assessment and treatment in neuropsychological rehabilitation. *Neuropsychology*, *5*, 281–291.

Wilson, B. A. (1991b). Long term prognosis of patients with severe memory disorders. *Neuropsychological Rehabilitation*, *1*, 117–134.

Wilson, B. A. (1991c). Behaviour therapy in the treatment of neurologically impaired adults. In P. R. Martin (Ed.), *Handbook of behavior therapy and psychological science: An integrative approach* (pp. 227–252). New York: Pergamon Press.

Wilson, B. A. (1992). Memory therapy in practice. In B. A. Wilson & N. Moffat (Eds.), *Clinical management of memory problems* (2nd ed., pp. 120–153). London: Chapman & Hall.

Wilson, B. A. (1996). La readaptation cognitive chez les cérébro-lésés. In M. I. Boatez (Ed.), Neuropsychologie Clinique et Neurologie du Comportement (2nd ed., pp. 637–652). Montreal: Les Presses de l'Universitie de Montreal.

Wilson, B. A. (1997a). Cognitive rehabilitation: How it is and how it might be. *Journal of the International Neuropsychological Society*, *3*, 487–496.

Wilson, B. A. (1997b). Management of acquired cognitive disorders. In B. A. Wilson & D. L. McLellan (Eds.), *Rehabilitation studies handbook* (pp. 243–261). Cambridge: Cambridge University Press.

Wilson, B. A. (1998). Recovery of cognitive functions following non-progressive brain injury. *Current Opinion in Neurobiology*, *8*, 281–287.

Wilson, B. A. (1999). *Case studies in neuropsychological rehabilitation*. New York: Oxford University Press.

Wilson, B. A., & Evans, J. J. (1996). Error free learning in the rehabilitation of individuals with memory impairments. *Journal of Head Trauma Rehabilitation*, *11*, 54–64.

Wilson, B. A., Alderman, N., Burgess, P., Emslie, H., & Evans, J. (1996). *Behavioural Assessment of the Dysexecutive Syndrome*. Bury St Edmunds, UK: Thames Valley Test Company.

Wilson, B. A., Baddeley, A. D., Evans, J. J., & Shiel, A. (1994). Errorless learning in the rehabilitation of memory impaired people. *Neuropsychological Rehabilitation*, *4*, 307–326.

Wilson, B. A., Baddeley, A., Shiel, A., & Patton, G. (1992). How does post traumatic amnesia differ from the amnesic syndrome and from chronic memory impairment? *Neuropsychological Rehabilitation*, *2*, 231–243.

Wilson, B. A., Carter, G., Norris, D., & Page, M. (2001a). Does errorless learning work through implicit or explicit memory? *Journal of the International Neuropsychological Society*, *7*, 250 (abstract).

Wilson, B. A., Cockburn, J., & Baddeley, A. D. (1985). *The Rivermead Behavioural Memory Test*. Bury St Edmunds, UK: Thames Valley Test Company.

Wilson, B. A., Cockburn, J., & Halligan, P. W. (1987). *The Behavioural Inattention Test*. Bury St Edmunds, UK: Thames Valley Test Company.

Wilson, B. A., Emslie, H. C., Quirk, K., & Evans, J. J. (2001b). Reducing everyday memory and planning problems by means of a paging system: A randomised control crossover study. *Journal of Neurology, Neurosurgery and Psychiatry*, *70*, 477–482.

Wilson, B. A., Evans, J., Brentnall, S., Bremner, S., Keohane, C., & Williams, H. (2000a). The Oliver Zangwill Centre for Neuropsychological Rehabilitation: A partnership between health care and rehabilitation research. In A.-L. Christensen & B. P. Uzzell (Eds.), *International handbook of neuropsychological rehabilitation* (pp. 231–246). New York: Kluwer Academic/Plenum Publishers.

Wilson, B. A., Evans, J. J., Emslie, H., Balleny, H., Watson, P. C., & Baddeley, A. D. (1999). Measuring recovery from post traumatic amnesia. *Brain Injury, 13*(7), 505–520.

Wilson, B. A., Evans, J. J., Emslie, H., & Malinek, V. (1997). Evaluation of NeuroPage: A new memory aid. *Journal of Neurology, Neurosurgery and Psychiatry, 63,* 113–115.

Wilson, B. A., Evans, J. J., & Keohane, C. (2002). Cognitive rehabilitation: A goal-planning approach with a man who sustained a head injury and cerebro-vascular complications. *Journal of Head Trauma Rehabilitation, 17,* 542–555.

Wilson, B. A., Evans, J. J., & Williams, H. (in press). Memory problems. In A. D. Tyerman (Ed.), *Rehabilitation after traumatic brain injury: A psychological approach.* Leicester, UK: The British Psychological Society.

Wilson, B. A., Watson, P. C., Baddeley, A. D., Emslie, H., & Evans, J. J. (2000b). Improvement or simply practice? The effects of twenty repeated assessments on people with and without brain injury. *Journal of the International Neuropsychological Society, 6,* 469–479.

Wilson, C., & Robertson, I. H. (1992). A home-based intervention for attentional slips during reading following head injury: A single case study. *Neuropsychological Rehabilitation, 2,* 193–205.

Wong, S. E., & Liberman, R. P. (1981). Mixed single-subject designs in clinical research: Variations of the multiple baseline. *Behavioural Assessment, 3,* 297–306.

Wood, R. L. (1984). Behaviour disorders following severe brain injury: Their presentation and psychological management. In D. N. Brooks (Ed.), *Closed head injury: Social, psychological and family consequences.* Oxford: Oxford University Press.

Wood, R. L. (1987). *Brain injury rehabilitation: A neurobehavioural approach.* London: Croom Helm.

Wood, R. L. (1988). Management of behaviour disorders in a day treatment setting. *Journal of Head Trauma Rehabilitation, 3,* 53–62.

Wood, R. L. (1990). *Neurobehavioural sequelae of traumatic brain injury.* London: Taylor & Francis Ltd.

Wood, R. L., & Eames, P. G. (1981). Application of behavioural modification of traumatically brain injured adults. In G. Davey (Ed.), *Application of conditioning theory* (pp. 81–101). London: Methuen.

Wood, R. L., & McMillan, T. M. (2000). *Neurobehavioural disability and social handicap after traumatic brain injury.* Hove, UK: Psychology Press.

Youngson, H., & Alderman, N. (1992). Fear of incontinence and its effects on a community based rehabilitation programme after severe brain injury: Successful remediation of escape behaviour using behaviour modification. *Brain Injury, 8,* 23–26.

Yuen, H. H., & Benzing, P. (1996). Guiding of behaviour through redirection in brain injury rehabilitation. *Brain Injury, 10,* 229–238.

Yule, W., & Carr, J. (Eds.). (1987). *Behaviour modification for people with mental handicaps* (2nd ed.). London: Croom Helm.

Yule, W., & Hemsley, D. (1977). Single case method in medical psychology. In S. Rachman (Ed.), *Contributions to medical psychology* (Vol. 1, pp. 211–299). New York: Pergamon Press.

Zasler, N. D., & Horn, L. J. (1990). Rehabilitative management of sexual dysfunction. *Journal of Head Trauma Rehabilitation, 5,* 14–24.

Zencius, A., & Wesolowski, M. D. (1989). Using stress management to decrease inappropriate behaviour in a brain-injured male. *Behavioural Residential Treatment, 5,* 61–64.

Zencius, A. H., & Wesolowski, M. D. (1999). Is the social network analysis necessary in the rehabilitation of individuals with head injury? *Brain Injury, 13,* 723–727.

Zencius, A., Wesolowski, M. D., Burke, W. H., & Hough, S. (1990). Managing hypersexual disorders in brain-injured clients. *Brain Injury*, *4*, 175–181.

Zencius, A., Wesolowski, M. D., Burke, W. H., & McQuaide, P. (1989). Antecedent control in the treatment of brain-injured clients. *Brain Injury*, *3*, 199–205.

Zigmond, A. S., & Snaith, R. P. (1983). The Hospital Anxiety and Depression Scale. *Acta Psychiatrica Scandinavica*, *67*, 361–370.

Zlutnick, S., Mayville, W. J., & Moffat, S. (1975). Modification of seizure disorders: The interruption of behavioral chains. *Journal of Applied Behavior Analysis*, *8*, 1–12.

Author Index

Subject Index